HOW SHALL THEY HEAR?

WHY NON-PREACHERS NEED TO KNOW WHAT PREACHING IS

RYAN M. MCGRAW

PRAISE FOR 'HOW SHALL THEY HEAR?'

Christian, either your prayers for preachers will call down heavenly power, or your prayerlessness will rob the church of a blessing. Do you pray for the preaching of God's Word? This insightful, much-needed book about preaching will teach you how. Read each chapter slowly and meditatively, turn its main ideas into prayers, and watch how God works.

— Dr. Joel R. Beeke, President, Puritan Reformed Theological Seminary, Grand Rapids, Michigan

While books on preaching abound, most of them should be avoided. They are more like 'How to' manuals than helpful and challenging essays on what the word of God has to teach us about preaching. Thankfully, Ryan McGraw has avoided this pitfall and given preachers *and* hearers a brief, helpful, stimulating and practical guide to the biblical principles and precepts that should indelibly shape the preaching of God's word. In fourteen brief chapters (each chapter is around six pages in length), McGraw asks fourteen searching questions e.g. What is preaching? How should preaching be done? What are the proper aims of preaching? What are the proper methods for preaching? (three chapters). What should preaching Christ look like? Each chapter helpfully concludes with a series of questions which seek to earth and further explicate the teaching. McGraw avoids giving the impression that there is one model for preachers to follow. He understands that preaching is deeply idiosyncratic, that preachers are all wired differently. What he does do, however, is to highlight and impress on preacher and hearer alike, the vital importance of preaching being shaped and styled, not by culture but by Scripture. One feature that is worthy of special comment is the attention McGraw gives to sermon hearers. He appreciates that preaching is a two way communication of God's truth and needs to be rightly heard as well as rightly preached. I heartily commend the book and trust it will become a 'vade mecum' for young would-be preachers in particular.

— IAN HAMILTON, INVERNESS, SCOTLAND

EP Books (Evangelical Press), Registered Office: 140 Coniscliffe Road, Darlington, Co Durham DL3 7RT

admin@epbooks.org

www.epbooks.org

EP Books are distributed in the USA by:

JPL Books, 3883 Linden Ave. S.E., Wyoming, MI 49548

order@jplbooks.com

www.jplbooks.com

© Ryan M McGraw 2019. All rights reserved.

British Library Cataloguing in Publication Data available

Print ISBN 978-1-78397-250-0

eBook ISBN 978-1-78397-251-7

Scripture taken from the New King James Version®. Copyright © 1982 by Thomas Nelson. Used by permission. All rights reserved.

To John and Pam Leding
Faithful friends in Christ whose fellowship, feedback, and encouragement the Lord has used to help me grow, both in my preaching and in my love for Christ.

CONTENTS

Introduction	ix
Acknowledgments	xv
1. What is Preaching?	1
2. Why is Preaching Necessary?	10
3. How Should Preaching be Done?	22
4. What are the Proper Aims of Preaching?	30
5. What are the Spirit's Aims in Preaching?	38
6. How Does Preaching Relate to the Missions of the Persons of the Trinity?	46
7. What are the Proper Methods for Preaching Christ? (1)	54
8. What are the Proper Methods for Preaching Christ? (2)	63
9. What Are the Proper Methods for Preaching Christ? (3)	72
10. What Should Preaching Christ Look Like?	79
11. Is Preaching Christ Always Inherent to Preaching?	87
12. What Should Sermon Application Look Like?	94
13. How Should All Christians Participate in Sermons?	102
14. What if I Sit Under Preaching that Does not Match the Biblical Model?	109
15. Conclusion	116
16. Appendix: Following Sermon Structure	120
Select Bibliography	127
Notes	131

INTRODUCTION

This book is a hard sell. Preaching is the primary means of grace, yet most Christians do not spend much time studying it. Many preachers do so only to know how to prepare sermons. Those who don't preach would rather study something else that they participate in, such as the sacraments. Some believers study how to preach, most don't study preaching at all, and very few study the theology of preaching. The result is that preachers often preach without asking how the Bible defines preaching, what agenda it sets for preaching, and what preaching should look like in light of these deeper questions. Likewise, non-preachers sit under the primary means of grace every week without understanding why it is the primary means of grace and why they should expect to hear Christ's voice through it.

Christ has used gospel preaching to expand his kingdom throughout the centuries and the preached Word has struck like lightning from heaven leaving the hearts of men and women aflame with faith, hope, and love. As Martyn Lloyd-Jones wrote, "You cannot read the history of the Church, even in a cursory manner, without seeing that preaching has always occupied a central and predominating position in the life of the Church, particularly in Protestantism."[1] Augustine came to Christ through Anselm's preaching. Bernard of Clairveaux sought to reform the church by founding an order of preachers. Thomas Aquinas wrote his theological masterpiece, the *Summa Theologiae*, to be a field guide for preachers. Martin Luther, John Calvin, John Knox, Heinrich Bullinger, and generations of Protestants after them sought reform primarily through preaching. The first Great Awakening saw revival through Spirit-filled preachers, and the story goes on. Jesus Christ, who is the founder of the church, the Savior of the world, and our all in all, devoted his life to preaching the gospel. He is the foundation, content, and model of preaching in all ages.[2]

Yet how many Christians have read books on what preaching is and how it should be done? Why should we, if, after all, preaching is a task that few Christians will be called to do? For that matter, how many preachers hack away at the task of preparing and delivering sermons without sharpening their tools first by studying the Bible's theology of preaching and the goals that Scripture sets for preaching? The result is that Christ's voice is garbled rather than clear, both in the preacher's preaching and in the hearer's listening. We need to know what Christ would say if we would speak as his ambassadors and if we would seek to hear him clearly through preaching.

While many believers recognize that preaching is the primary means through which Christ calls his people to the Father by the Spirit's work in their hearts, books on preaching generally sell more poorly than books on prayer or on baptism and the Lord's Supper. Sadly, though even more certainly, books on preaching sell worse than books on Christian dieting. It is easiest to neglect that which is in plain sight; that which is most important is often least understood, especially when we think it is less controversial and that we get it already. Good preaching is often the primary criteria visitors use in choosing which church to join, yet how do they know what good preaching is if they don't prayerfully search the Bible for answers? It is important, therefore, for all Christians to know what preaching is and why it matters. Through preaching, Christ speaks to his church by his Word and Spirit today.

In order to recover the power of preaching in the church and the world, preachers and hearers alike need to ask in light of Scripture, what is preaching?

Who is this book written for and why?

This book aims to help all Christians understand what preaching is, how it should be done, and why they have a vested interest in it. It is only indirectly a homiletical manual for pastors; directly, it is a guide to believers. It addresses preachers primarily insofar as they are believers who happen to preach. All of the chapters are short and many of them revolve around specific passages in the New Testament. These passages are memorable and the chapter outlines follow them closely. My goal is that even if you don't remember anything else I say, the Holy Spirit will burn these texts into your minds and hearts. Ultimately, this book seeks to help believers learn to love Christ better through hearing sermons.

From a preacher's standpoint, John Piper's *Expository Exultation* and the last third of Sinclair Ferguson's *Some Pastors and Teachers* say much of what I want to say in this book with greater spiritual skill and rich experience. What makes this present book stand out is that it takes the same ideas (my own as well!) about preaching but seeks to bring them to a different audience. It is beyond time that non-preachers study preaching as the primary means of grace.

The study questions at the close of each chapter have two goals. First, to guide as to how well understood the Bible's teaching on preaching is, and the main points made in each chapter. Second, to apply each text personally and interpersonally. My hope is that this will make this book not only necessary for non-preachers, but ideal for promoting discussions about preaching among non-preachers, seeking to bring each biblical text and its teachings home to individuals and to churches.

What does this book include?

Each chapter begins with a question about preaching. I ask questions that the Bible raises about preaching and I seek to let the Bible answer them. Sometimes the questions that God teaches us that we should have are more important than those we come up with on our own. I have chosen texts that answer the questions raised directly. The first six chapters answer these questions by seeking to allow six passages of Scripture to be heard with their own voice. This material unfolds what preaching is, why it is necessary, how it should be done, its general aims, the Spirit's aims in relation to Christ, and how preaching relates to the work of the Triune God. These chapters provide the framework for all subsequent chapters because the nature and design of preaching treated in them shapes what sermons should look like. This material shows that there is much more involved in sermons than merely explaining texts of Scripture. The Holy Spirit has given a Christ-exalting agenda for preaching that is the ground on which every sermon stands and the atmosphere in which preachers and hearers breathe. The next three chapters describe some of the tools that preachers should use in order to achieve the biblical goals of preaching. This is important in helping non-preachers know what to expect in preaching. Two chapters follow that present biblical examples of preaching Christ from the apostle Paul and from passages of Scripture that lead to challenges in preaching. The last two chapters of the book apply the teaching of earlier chapters by showing all Christians their role in relation to preaching and how to address difficulties that arise in relation to preaching and to listening to sermons. The appendix seeks to help hearers listen to sermons well by illustrating how to identify purpose and structure in sermons.

Every chapter, the appendix excepted, began as a post

on the blog Reformation 21. I have expanded and edited this material to put it in book format with the permission of the Alliance of Confessing Evangelicals.

What should I do with this book?

The Spirit's ultimate aim in preaching is to make Christ heard over the noise and distractions of the world, the flesh, and the devil. We need to hear Christ in order to know him and to call on him. We need to hear his Father reaching out to us in the sermon and calling us home. His Son is the path home and his Spirit gives us the spiritual legs of faith to walk on. The church needs both good preachers and good hearers. As listeners, we need to understand what is going on in sermons, what to expect, and why we are there. Christ will continue to use preaching, among other means, to spread his kingdom and to speak to his church. My hope is that this book will help all readers to love Christ more through the preached Word. When you hear Christ's Word preached, can you hear his voice in the words?

Ryan M. McGraw

Morton H. Smith Professor of Systematic Theology, Greenville Presbyterian Theological Seminary. Adjunct Professor of Doctoral Studies, Puritan Reformed Theological Seminary.

ACKNOWLEDGMENTS

Some friends who are not preachers offered invaluable help in setting the parameters for these studies. In particular, Brad Hettervik, Marco Ribeiro, and Tim Daniels helped me think through questions listeners often have about preaching, including what goes into preparing sermons, whether preaching runs the risk of becoming merely academic, how the pastor profits from preaching, how people can listen to sermons better, what the theology of preaching is, how to prepare for and apply sermons, and how to involve children in sermons. Questions like these both confirmed and expanded the direction that I intended to go with this book. Adam Richwine also raised some important questions regarding the place of preaching in the life and ministry of the local church.

I thank my Sunday school class at Covenant Community Orthodox Presbyterian Church in Taylors, SC for discussing these texts and issues with interest, zeal, and love for Christ. I also thank my seminary students who have both heard me preach and lecture on these issues, as I begged the Spirit to make up for my deficiencies and to help them learn better than I can teach. However, I am most grateful to faithful believers in Belem, Brazil and those who attended the Os Puritanos Symposium in Maragogi in 2018. And thank you to Manuel Canuto for inviting me to come (twice!). It is a great privilege to play a small part in this work, by the grace of the Triune God. Even through a translator, we experienced the presence and power of the Spirit, who exalted Christ to the Father's glory while I had the privilege of preaching many of the texts in this book. These conferences represent the exact audience that I am targeting in this book. My prayer is that the Triune God would bless the written form of this material a fraction of the degree to which he blessed myself and the other speakers as we preached about preaching in Brazil. May the Lord use such means to spark revival in Brazil as well as in my own country through means like these.

Nick Batzig deserves thanks for asking me to write regularly for Reformation 21. As I prayed over what to write, this book virtually spilled out of my heart into my computer. I thank the Alliance of Confessing Evangelicals for allowing me to reuse and to expand this material significantly in book form.

Several friends read a draft of this material and enriched it through useful feedback. I am grateful in particular to Ian Hamilton, Peyton Jones, Marco Ribeiro, and Ben Castle for reading and commenting on early drafts. In particular, Marco and Ben's extensive comments and constructive criticism enriched the work greatly, particularly in relation to clarity and application. Evelyn MacIntrye provided great help with the book title, as well as enthusiasm for the project.

As always, my wife Krista has been a continual encouragement. She lives with my projects as she shares life with me; she showed particular enthusiasm for this book. Owen, Calvin, Jonathan, and Callie are always a joyful part of our lives as well. They received most of the contents of the book in family worship and in following me to various churches as I have preached and taught these things as many times as the Lord has given me the opportunity to do so. I thank the Lord for you all and I would be a poorer pastor, preacher, professor, and writer without you.

1

WHAT IS PREACHING?

Now then, we are ambassadors for Christ, as though God were pleading through us: we implore *you* on Christ's behalf, be reconciled to God. For He made Him who knew no sin *to be* sin for us, that we might become the righteousness of God in Him. We then, *as* workers together *with Him* also plead with *you* not to receive the grace of God in vain. For He says: "In an acceptable time I have heard you, and in the day of salvation I have helped you." Behold, now *is* the accepted time; behold, now *is* the day of salvation.

— 2 Corinthians 5:20-6:2

In 2018, my wife and I traveled to Brazil for two weeks so that I could preach two conferences in two cities. We left our children with her family in the USA. One night, our ten-year-old son took it upon himself to "help" his three-year-old sister go to bed. He told her when it was time to go to bed, he helped her get ready for bed, and he put her in the bed. She always went to bed for mom and dad, yet she did not listen to her brother. While he used the same words that mom and dad used to put his sister to bed, she knew that he did not have the authority to speak in the place of mom and dad. The next night we called my wife's sister and authorized her to enforce the rules with our three year old and we told our daughter about the arrangement. Suddenly everything changed. Even though my sister-in-law used the same words that that our son had used, she spoke on behalf of mom and dad and our daughter listened. If she had not listened, then she would have faced the same consequences that she would if she had rejected mom and dad's commands directly.

This is somewhat like preaching. Preaching uses words. Yet words alone do not make preaching. Not even God's words are enough to constitute preaching, for preaching involves an ambassador who is authorized to speak in someone else's place. Not all gospel communication, vital though it is, is preaching. Preaching comes through an ambassador who is authorized to speak on Christ's behalf and through whom God pleads with sinners. In preaching, we hear God's voice, in Christ, by the Spirit in a way that is comparable to hearing a message through a message bearer.

Defining preaching

In order to study preaching well, we need to define it. Good teaching begins with definitions. Effective schoolteachers tell their students what they are doing and why in order to help students learn well. This often means defining terms specific to each subject. Math students need to learn what a hypotenuse is and students of physics need to understand what mass, acceleration, and velocity mean. The Bible also has its own vocabulary, which includes "preaching."[1] Yet many Christians sit under sermons, and some even preach them, without a working definition of what preaching is in light of Scripture.

While the term "preaching" does not appear in the passage cited above, it describes the task of preachers. Some passages of the Bible use Greek words for "preaching." Others teach us about preaching even when the word is not there. Still others help us learn what to expect from the Triune God in preaching in light of how he works in sinner's hearts more generally. This passage fits in the second category. While the term preaching is not in the text, the passage describes the role of one of the best preachers of all time. Paul's self-description as an ambassador of Christ results in a long definition of preaching: Preaching is a public, authoritative proclamation of the gospel, through ordained ambassadors of Christ, who plead with people to be reconciled to God on Christ's behalf, on the grounds of Christ's person and work. The short version is that it is a public, authoritative proclamation of the gospel. The longer answer builds a fuller sight of preaching that walks through the text like climbing stairs until we get a complete view of preaching from the top. Each section below will explain this definition in light of this text. Understanding what preaching is helps us understand its purposes and what we should expect when listening to sermons. This is important because Christ designed preaching to be an ordinary part of evangelism and discipleship (Matthew 28:19-20).

Christ's messengers

This text teaches us what preaching is. Preaching is a public, authoritative proclamation of the gospel. Preaching cannot be done in private. Talking to a friend about the gospel is not preaching. Paul's preaching was public proclamation. He implored people and he pleaded with them "on Christ's behalf." His self-description as an "ambassador" meant that his preaching carried authority. Whether referring to the twelve apostles (Matthew 10:5-15) or to the seventy whom Christ sent (Luke 10:1-12), Christ's words apply: "He who receives you receives Me, and he who receives Me receives Him who sent Me" (Matthew 10:40). Preachers implore sinners and plead with them on Christ's behalf. This is how they "do the work of an evangelist" (2 Timothy 4:5). Preaching is "the ministry of reconciliation" (2 Corinthians 5:18) through which Christ's pleads with us and implores us through his messengers. When we receive the message of Christ's ambassadors, then we receive Christ. When we reject their message, then we reject the Christ whom they preach. This is true with respect to all faithful gospel preaching, which we will see below. Preaching comes with the authority of Christ through his ambassadors and we must submit to Christ through it.

Authorized ambassadors

We also learn here who preachers are. All Americans are citizens and represent their country, but not all Americans are ambassadors who can speak on behalf of the country. Similarly, preachers are ordained ambassadors of Christ. In 2 Corinthians, Paul defended his ministry at length against false apostles (2 Corinthians 2:17, 11:5). In doing so, he not only defined the nature and purposes of his apostolic ministry, but he established the pattern of gospel ministry more broadly.

Being an ambassador implies gifting, calling, and ordination. I will address ordination more fully in the next chapter in relation to Romans 10:14-17. Preaching is defined primarily in relation to office. Christ gifts church officers for their office and he gives officers as gifts to his church. Ephesians 4:11 teaches that the ascended Christ gave apostles, prophets, evangelists, pastors, and teachers as gifts to his church. Some of these teaching offices were extraordinary and temporary while others are ordinary and permanent. Yet all of them instruct the church for its purity and unity, its maturity and growth in Christ, and its protection from false teaching (Ephesians 4:12-16).

Although it is not always clear in English translations, the New Testament sometimes distinguishes authorized preaching through ordained officers from the general evangelistic efforts of all Christians by using different

Greek terms for each. For example, Luke wrote that believers in general evangelized (*euangelidzomai*) as they were scattered abroad, but Philip preached (*keruso*) Christ (Acts 8:4-5). All teaching offices come from Christ and revolve around proclaiming his person and work. Christ preached the kingdom of God (Mark 1:39).

Only those authorized by Christ should preach. When Christ cleansed a leper, warning him to tell no one (Mark 1:40-44), the man preached (*keruso*) without being gifted, called, and ordained (v. 45). He attempted to preach without being called to preach. The result was that Jesus could no longer "openly enter the city" (v. 45). Well-meaning people who try to preach without proper calling and ordination may end up unintentionally doing more harm than good. All Christians must evangelize, yet not all are permitted to preach. All Christians are Christ's servants, but not all Christians are Christ's ambassadors.[2]

Christ-appointed and Christ-based

We learn next why Christ appointed preaching and preachers. Preaching is simultaneously like a suitor wooing his beloved, like a judge summoning a criminal to give an account, and like a king pleading with his enemies to make peace with him before he destroys them. Preachers plead with people on Christ's behalf to be reconciled to God. Preaching flows from the fear of the Lord in preparing people for the final judgment (2 Corinthians 5:9-11). The love of Christ compels sound preaching (v. 12-15). Preaching seeks to provide a true view of God's saving aims through his person and work (v. 16-19). Preaching is God's act of calling sinners to be reconciled to him through Christ (v. 20, 6:1-2). As we must define preaching in relation to office, so the Christ, who is the source of church offices, directs both the motives behind and the content of preaching.

Lastly, preaching is founded on Christ's person and work. The gospel is not a list of benefits that we receive any more than marriage is the money or possessions that a wife brings into the relationship. Jesus Christ is the gospel and there is no good news apart from him, no matter how rich the dowry appears. Preaching is possible because God was in Christ reconciling the world to himself (2 Corinthians 5:19). Preaching proclaims Christ's person and work for the salvation of all (v. 21).

God reconciles sinners to himself in Christ because Christ is fully God, enabling him to match God's infinite majesty and the infinite weight of sin. Equally necessary, he is fully man, enabling him to obey, suffer, die, and rise in his human nature for us. God becoming man alone could enable God to purchase the church with his own blood (Acts 20:28). Christ became sin for sinners, removing God's wrath and curse from them, so that sinners might become the righteousness of God in him, being justified freely through him (2 Corinthians 5:21; Romans 3:24).

Christ gifts and calls preachers to be his ambassadors by virtue of his ascension (Ephesians 4:8). The Holy Spirit is like the best man at a wedding who has no greater joy than to see the bride and groom come together in marriage. Preachers are both like the groomsmen witnessing the marriage and instruments that the Spirit uses to apply Christ to men and women's hearts. Christ makes preaching possible through making himself the ground of the message preached. We must receive Christ by faith through preaching as he presents himself to us through his ambassadors.

This passage helps us understand what preaching is both negatively and positively. Negatively, by implication, not all gospel proclamation is preaching. Neither does all preaching have the right object. Preaching must impart the whole counsel of God (Acts 20:27) in a way that demonstrates that all of the promises of God are yes and amen in Christ (2 Corinthians 1:20). Positively, preaching is the public, authoritative proclamation of the gospel through ordained ambassadors of Christ. Preachers plead with people to be reconciled to God on the grounds of Christ's person and work. Preaching is Christ's ordinary means of seeking and saving the lost. This means that there is continuity in how preaching addresses believers as well as the unconverted.

Paul implored Christians at Corinth "not to receive the grace of God in vain." Christ is set forth in preaching to believers and to unbelievers alike because the accepted day of salvation is a perpetual "now." As John Chrysostom wrote, "Let us therefore not let slip away the favorable opportunity but display a zeal worthy of the grace."[3] All subsequent chapters in this book expand and explain the ideas presented here. We must understand what preaching is in order to understand how and why we should listen to sermons. Do we receive Christ through his ordained ambassadors as we press onward and upward towards the culmination of our salvation in Christ (Philippians 3:14)?

～

Study Questions

1. What is the short definition of preaching? What is the longer definition? Why are the parts of this longer definition important for understanding what preaching is?
2. Why is 2 Corinthians 5:20-6:2 an important text about preaching, even though the term "preaching" is not in the text?
3. What does it mean to be an ambassador? How does this idea affect our view of preaching?
4. If not all Christians are preachers, then why should we all evangelize the lost? What are some ways that we can pursue evangelism even though we are not called to be preachers?
5. How should we prepare to hear the preaching of the Word? Does it make a difference to regard the preacher as Christ's ambassador?

2

WHY IS PREACHING NECESSARY?

How then shall they call on Him in whom they have not believed? And how shall they believe in Him of whom they have not heard? And how shall they hear without a preacher? And how shall they preach unless they are sent? As it is written: "How beautiful are the feet of those who preach the gospel of peace, who bring glad tidings of good things!" But they have not all obeyed the gospel. For Isaiah says, "Lord, who has believed our report?" So then faith *comes* by hearing, and hearing by the word of God.

— ROMANS 10:14-17

The means of salvation

Our family drives from South Carolina to California at least once a year to visit family. We try to make sure our vehicle is safe before going on such a long trip. We need to make sure that the car has oil. We need to inflate the tires and check the engine. There are things to do to keep us safe during the trip as well. We need to put gas in the car periodically. We need to make sure that the drivers are well fed and rested (and have coffee available). We have to watch out for other drivers. Yet ultimately, we are not safe until we reach California, pull into the driveway, and turn the car off. This is similar to the relationship between preaching and our salvation. Preaching is God's primary means of saving sinners safely to God from the beginning, through the middle, and to the end of the Christian life.

Salvation essentially means "safety." Salvation includes the application of Christ's work from the new birth, through faith and repentance, to justification, adoption, sanctification, and glorification. Christians share in Christ's benefits because they are united to him through faith and they enjoy communion in those benefits. We have been saved (Ephesians 2:8), we are being saved (2 Corinthians 2:15), and we shall be saved (Romans 5:9). God uses means such as the Word, the sacraments, and prayer to save sinners (Westminster Shorter Catechism 88). We receive Christ by faith as we use his appointed means to foster and to exercise our faith.

Another way to look at this issue is to ask the question: "Is reading the Bible in private enough to save us?" Not ultimately. Like the Bereans, we must receive the preached Word "with all readiness" and we must search the Scriptures daily "to find out whether these things [are] so" (Acts 17:11). Preaching is ordinarily a necessary means for salvation because it is the ordinary means through which we hear Christ and are saved by him. Romans 10:14-17 explains why preaching is necessary, who should do it, what it proclaims, its opposition, and its purpose. These truths show us why we need preaching as a means of promoting our salvation through union and communion with Christ.

Hearing the Lord Jesus Christ

Preaching is necessary because people need to hear Christ in order to believe in him for salvation. There can be several true answers to a single question. For example, someone may have a child who does not play soccer. If a friend asks them why the child does not play soccer, then they can say that the child was not chosen for the team. They can also say that the child did not want to play. However, they might also say that the child was not yet old enough for the team and that the story may be different in the future. Similarly, Romans 9-11 answers the question why so many Jews did not receive Christ as their Messiah.

Paul answered this question in at least three ways. In chapter 9, he wrote that not all Jews came to faith because God did not choose to save all of them. Chapter 11 concludes that God preserved an elect remnant of ethnic Jews now, such as Paul, and that he would save many more of them in the future. Chapter 10 explains that unbelieving Jews were also guilty because they chose to reject Christ. Paul responded to this situation by teaching that God saves both Jews and Gentiles through preaching. He pressed the necessity of preaching in light of the fact that people need to call upon Christ through faith. Circumcised Jews needed to be circumcised in heart (Jeremiah 9:25-26; Romans 2:28-29).

Uncircumcised Gentiles "were without Christ, being aliens from the commonwealth of Israel and strangers from the covenants of promise, having no hope and without God in the world" (Ephesians 2:12). Only Christ's blood could bring both Jews and Gentiles near to God (v13-18). Paul added that it was not enough to hear about Christ. People need to hear Christ's voice. The Greek text of Romans 10:14 says literally, "How shall they believe him whom they have not heard? And how shall they hear [him] without a preacher?" As Christ spoke in Paul (2 Corinthians 13:3), and as Christ pleads with sinners through his ambassadors (2 Corinthians 5:20), so people hear Christ through preachers in order to believe Christ himself.

This does not mean that Christ does not call people through Bible reading and that he does not use the sacraments and prayer as means of salvation. Yet preaching is the ordinary means by which we must learn Christ and hear his voice (Ephesians 4:20). How God can save sinners and how he ordinarily chooses to do so are different questions. When we listen to sermons, we should expect to hear Christ in the sermon as he calls us to himself by his Word and Spirit.

Appointed messengers

Preaching comes through Christ's sent messengers. If two nations are at war and they suddenly call for a truce, then someone must bear the news. If the troops on the front lines are the only ones to spread the news, then most of the army on the field will not know what to believe. Without sending authorized messengers to bear the good news confusion will result and peace will be more like a rumor than a reality. The text implies that preachers are necessary for preaching and that God must equip and send them to preach on Christ's behalf. If preaching is necessary, then so are preachers. This point builds upon the previous chapter, which defined preaching as a public authoritative proclamation of the gospel through Christ's ordained ambassadors.

To identify preaching we must identify preachers properly. We saw that Christ gifts preachers through the Spirit. Christ sends preachers to do their work by calling them into office through the church. He calls men to serve as officers through the election of the congregation and the laying on of hands by a group of elders (presbytery, in Greek. Acts 1:23, 6:3-6, 14:23; 1 Timothy 4:14). This former act is election and latter is ordination. The church recognizes the gifts of those whom Christ is sending to preach; it does not give gifts to them. As Martyn Lloyd-Jones wrote, "Preachers are born, not made."[1] As D. B. Knox summarized, "Ordination is recognition of God-given ministry by the congregation led by its spiritual leaders."[2]

This reinforces the idea that we must define preaching largely in terms of office. We should seek to hear and receive Christ through the preaching of those preachers whom he has sent.

Proclaiming good news

Preaching is necessary because it brings to us glad tidings from God. This affects the tone of preaching. We may expect a funeral director to be somber while conducting a funeral. However, we expect an MC at a wedding to be full of joy and energy. Preaching is good news and those who preach should be full of good cheer, excitement, zeal, and Spirit-filled joy. Paul cited Isaiah 52:7 to show the blessedness of those who bring "the gospel of peace." "Gospel" means "good news" and proclaiming this good news is inherent to preaching. This means that preaching has a positive aim. It is the "sweet savor of Christ" to God (2 Corinthians 2:15 KJV) and God intends preaching to be the "savor of life unto life" to those who believe (v. 16). Preaching should have a positive tone because Christ's person and work are its objects. In preaching, we hear the voice of the Christ who saves.

Surely this means that preaching is not simply lifelessly reading a paper to a captive audience who have to take it, like bad tasting medicine, because they know it is good for them. Preachers should be excited to preach Christ because he is the content of their message, he is the true messenger, and he is the Savior of those receiving the message.

Life or death?

Yet the positive aim of preaching often meets opposition. Parents who try to wean their children off sugar because it contributes to severe health problems like cavities, diabetes, obesity, and even cancer will meet resistance. The children hear only a threat of taking away something that they love instead of a promise of a healthier and happier life in the long run.

In spite of the positive message of preaching, Paul cited Isaiah 53:1 to show that preaching does not always bring life. The preached Word becomes a "savor of death" to those who reject Christ (2 Corinthians 2:16KJV). It was so to unbelieving Israel in Isaiah's day, it was so to unbelieving Jews in Paul's day, and it remains so to all people who refuse Christ's voice through preaching today. Preaching condemns incidentally; its aim is to save rather than to condemn.

Preaching announces God's love in sending his Son to save those who believe (John 3:16). He did not send him to condemn the world, but to save it (v. 17). Preaching condemns only those who do not believe in the only begotten Son of God (v. 18). People bring their own darkness to bear on the gospel, the nature of which is light (v. 19). Those who love darkness hate light and shun its radiance (v. 20). Yet those who love the truth as it is in Jesus (Ephesians 4:21) love the light that he is and brings.

The darkness in people's hearts leads them to flee the light, but the darkness of the world cannot overcome the light (John 1:5). God will achieve the end of calling people out of darkness into his marvelous light (1 Peter 2:9) and he will use preaching as a means of doing so.

Staying on track

Preachers and hearers must be careful at this juncture. For example, have you ever been tempted to say that the reason why people do not like the preaching in your local church is simply because the pastor preaches God's holiness and God's law, and people just don't like such things? This may be true, but it is also true that preachers can preach lawful things unlawfully, or improperly. Do we desire to hear the law because we want sermons to be convicting? Or do we want to be convicted so that the Spirit can put the character of God and of Jesus Christ on display before us? Do we want to hear the law so that we can have a list of rules to follow in every circumstance we face? Or do we want to hear it so that we can obey from the heart the form of doctrine that we have received (Romans 6:17)? Do we want to hear about God's holiness because we think that so many people are "irreverent" in our churches today? Or do we revel in God's holiness because the Christ, who was "holy, harmless, undefiled, [and] separate from sinners" (Hebrews 7:26) sanctifies us and perfects us forever through offering himself for our sins? (Hebrews 10:14). For instance, we can have (and preach) Sabbath keeping in heart, speech, and behavior in perfect agreement with Scripture and lose the Bible's emphasis and accent in delighting in the day for God's sake and as a means of hasting Christ's return in glory.

The line between the Pharisees and ourselves is not always marked by teaching God's law alone versus adding to his commandments. Sometimes it is preaching the law while losing sight of its inward spiritual qualities and without conjoining it with the positive thrust of gospel preaching. This is why the letter kills and the Spirit gives life (2 Corinthians 3:6). Do we recognize that though the gospel will condemn some (just like Paul's preaching did!), this is never the end of gospel preaching, which is to exalt the good news of God in Christ, with the Spirit's help?

Faith comes through hearing…

Preaching is necessary as the primary means that Christ uses to bring people to salvation because it promotes saving faith in Christ through hearing Christ himself. "Faith comes by hearing, and hearing by the word of God" (Romans 10:17). Some manuscripts read, "the word of Christ," instead of, "the word of God." In either case, Paul teaches us that preaching is the primary means of saving sinners because we hear Christ through preaching. Christ must, therefore, be the primary object of preaching.

Though preaching is defined partly in terms of office, Christ's work in sending preachers defines preaching in terms of its content as well. Chrysostom wrote, "You see how by the kind of preaching [Paul] points out the preacher. For there was nothing else that these men went about telling everywhere, but those unspeakable good things, and the peace made by God with men."[3]

Christ commissions preachers, they speak on Christ's behalf, and Christ speaks through them, in order that they should unfold the unsearchable riches of Christ (Ephesians 3:8). Failing to preach Christ in a sermon denies the definition and nature of preaching. Christian sermons must be distinctively Christian. Do we listen to sermons expecting to hear and receive Christ through them?

Does preaching really save?

Some will object at this stage that most of the Christians they know were not converted through preaching. They were either saved through the witness of a friend, through Bible reading, or through listening to sermons or podcasts online. The first thing that we need to grapple with is whether or not Paul says that preaching is necessary for salvation? If this is the case, then our experience must conform to Scripture rather than Scripture to our experience.

Retaining a broader meaning of salvation (past, present, and future) may help us here. The issue is not how we were converted or how we came to Christ, but whether preaching is ordinarily a necessary means through which we hear Christ's voice for our salvation. Ordinarily, preaching will permeate the Christian life from beginning to end. The Lord uses Bible reading, witnessing, and mp3 files to save sinners and we should use and recommend all of these things.

However, if it is really true that most people are not converted nor do they come to full and final salvation through preaching in our day, then maybe this says more about the current state of preaching than it does about preaching itself. We need to pursue safety in the Lord. We should expect preaching to be the primary vehicle to bring us safely to full and final salvation. Do we believe this? Does it affect how we hear sermons? Does it drive us to pray for good preaching and for godly preachers?

Study Questions

1. What does "salvation" mean in Scripture? How does our definition of salvation affect how we understand preaching as a necessary means for salvation?
2. What does it mean that we hear Christ in preaching? How can we expect to hear Christ's voice in preaching even if the preaching is not ideal?
3. How can we promote the importance of preaching in our personal evangelism?
4. What is the difference between listening to a sermon online and sitting under preaching on Sunday morning? What if the preachers we

listen to online are more gifted than those preaching in our local churches?
5. How should the positive goal of preaching affect the content and delivery of sermons? How does this affect our hearing? How does this result to the different personalities of preachers?

3

HOW SHOULD PREACHING BE DONE?

And I, brethren, when I came to you, did not come with excellence of speech or of wisdom declaring to you the testimony of God. For I determined not to know anything among you except Jesus Christ and Him crucified. I was with you in weakness, in fear, and in much trembling. And my speech and my preaching *were* not with persuasive words of human wisdom, but in demonstration of the Spirit and of power, that your faith should not be in the wisdom of men but in the power of God.

— 1 Corinthians 2:1-5

Spirit-filled preaching is arresting, even if listeners cannot explain why. Before coming to Christ, a friend of mine was invited by some of his friends to hear a well-known evangelical pastor. While he went into the church expecting nothing, he left the service astonished. He could not believe that the pastor and the people in the church believed that the people and events in the Old Testament were real. That afternoon, he found out that this pastor was going to be preaching again that evening and he asked his Christian friends if they wanted to go back again. Sadly, they had plans to watch a football game instead and the unbeliever went back to church by himself.

Eventually he came to Christ under the preaching of the Word. While he did not recognize it at the time, he was experiencing the Spirit's power under the preaching of the Word. His friends illustrate something important about the Holy Spirit's work in preaching as well. The Spirit works in preachers and in hearers, though he doesn't necessarily work in preachers or hearers in the same measure or even at the same time.

Apostolic preaching

Paul teaches us in 1 Corinthians 2:1-5 that preachers must preach Christ in demonstration of the Spirit and of power. This truth both informs the content of preaching and shapes the manner in which ministers ought to preach. We learn several vital lessons here about what preaching is not, about what it is, and about the proper manner of preaching.

Preaching must not be based on worldly speech or worldly wisdom. Paul contrasted excellence of speech and wisdom with preaching Christ and him crucified. The gospel message results in a paradox. While its message is foolishness to those who are perishing (1 Corinthians 1:18), it is the wisdom and the power of God to those who believe (v. 24). People cannot know God through worldly wisdom (v. 21) because when they profess to be wise apart from the true knowledge of the true God then they become fools (Romans 1:22). This is why God chose the "foolishness" of preaching to save those who believe (1 Corinthians 1:21).

Paul's point is not that Christ is foolish. Neither does he imply that preachers should not preach well or that sermons should be boring. Christ's preaching certainly was not boring.[1] We eat food because we need food to nourish our bodies, but we also thank the Lord when food tastes good. So, we should not be satisfied with boring dispassionate sermons that, technically, keep our souls alive while leaving a bad taste in our mouths. If the food we serve is good food, then we should enjoy it and help others enjoy it too.

Spurgeon wrote, "If with the zeal of Methodists, we can preach the doctrine of Puritans a great future is before us."[2] Paul is saying that preaching avoids worldly content and worldly methods because its content is the wisdom of God in Christ and its methods aim to preach the wisdom of God clearly. Though the world regards this as foolishness it is divine wisdom for salvation. Poison cooked well is poison still, but a good chef knows how to bring out the best flavors in the best foods. Likewise, God's wisdom in Christ informs the content and the manner of preaching.

Pleading with sinners

Preaching must have Christ as its primary object. As the last two chapters illustrated, 2 Corinthians 5:19-21 and Romans 10:14-17 teach that Christ pleads with sinners through preaching and that preaching aims to produce and foster faith in Christ. This is why in 1 Corinthians 2:2 Paul wrote that he intended to preach nothing other than Christ and him crucified.

The aim of preaching is to preach the gospel and Christ is the substance of the gospel. God made Christ wisdom from God, and righteousness, sanctification, and redemption so that he who boasts should boast in the Lord (1 Corinthians 1:30-31). "Christ crucified" is shorthand for Christ's work on our behalf. The Book of Acts frequently summarizes the gospel in terms of Christ's resurrection as well (e.g. Acts 17:31). Christ's humiliation descended to the deepest valley in his death. Christ's exaltation ascended to the highest summit in his resurrection. Preaching must proclaim "the whole counsel of God" (Acts 20:27), but it can do so only through the lens of Christ crucified and risen.

This does not mean that Christ is the only thing that preachers proclaim. We must be Christocentric and not Christomonistic.[3] This means that Christ is central to what we talk about without becoming the only thing that we talk about. However, preaching Christ is both part of the definition of preaching and it determines the manner of preaching. As William Perkins said, summarizing his instructions to preachers, "The heart of the matter is this:

preach one Christ, by Christ, to the praise of Christ."[4] Preaching is from Christ, through Christ, and to Christ because preaching is the primary means through which the Father brings us to himself through his Word and Spirit.

The power of the Holy Spirit

Preaching must be in demonstration of the Spirit and of power (1 Corinthians 2:4).[5] The Spirit's power in preaching is connected to the content of preaching. Preaching must proclaim God's Word rather than man's word. Preachers must proclaim the wisdom of God which eye has not seen, nor ear heard, nor has entered into the heart of man (1 Corinthians 2:6-9). These are not the hidden things of the future, but the revealed things of the present (v. 10, 13). The Spirit reveals God through Christ through divine revelation.

Yet preaching in the Spirit's power involves not only proclaiming the Spirit's revelation of God in Christ. Ministers need the Spirit to work to change hearers through conversion, growth, and perseverance. They need the Spirit to enflame their own hearts with love to the Christ whom they preach as well. Through receiving the Spirit of God, believers receive spiritual things, with spiritual discernment, for the spiritual knowledge of Christ (1 Corinthians 2:12-16).

Preaching in demonstration of the Spirit and of power is tied inextricably to preaching Christ and him crucified.[6] A Christless sermon is a Spiritless sermon. The

Spirit blesses preaching Christ in order to make the hearts of believers echo what he has revealed about Christ. This does not mean that a Christ-filled sermon is a Spirit-filled sermon, however. The Spirit is sovereign and he works at different times in different measures in different people. The gospel is more than good content. It is about knowing God, based on the promises of God in Christ, by the power of God's Spirit. While the Spirit does not always work in the same measure, preachers and hearers alike must pray for his blessing on their preaching and hearing. As we will see in a later chapter, by faith, they should also expect his presence and blessing.

Preaching in demonstration of the Spirit's power is like a properly functioning car. Cars are useful. They are vehicles designed to move us around. Yet however well constructed and attractive a car may be, it is useless without fuel. A car is also different than a gas motor. A motor may have fuel without being a vehicle. Likewise, preaching is a vehicle that requires fuel. God designed preaching to bring us to himself through faith in Christ. If preaching has the right content, yet the Holy Spirit is absent from it, then it becomes a vehicle without fuel. If preaching does not have the right content, then it becomes more like a motor than a vehicle, since it can no longer take us where we need to go. Only when the Spirit shapes the content of the sermon and blesses the act of preaching does preaching become a vehicle to bring us to God, through Christ, by the Spirit.

This passage leads to several important conclusions about preaching. We need the Holy Spirit in order to make preaching effective. Al Martin noted that the Spirit's "agency and operations in the act of preaching are an indispensable necessity for every preacher of the Word of God if his ministry would meet the biblical standard for what preaching ought to be."[7] We should pray for the Spirit's blessing on the preaching and the hearing of the gospel.

Preachers must cull from their sermons everything that does not pertain to the Spirit's power in preaching. Rhetoric in preaching is a means of making preaching an effective vehicle of communicating the gospel clearly in order to bring us to God. It is not an end in itself. We must filter all sermons through the goal of preaching Christ and him crucified.

Preachers must preach the whole counsel of God in relation to Christ. Preaching must be done in demonstration of the Spirit and of power and preaching Christ and him crucified is the means through which the Spirit exercises his power. These facts should create an expectation in listeners as we pray for the Spirit to bless us through preachers.

∽

Study Questions

1. Can you think of times in which the Holy Spirit has blessed you greatly under the preaching of the Word? How is the Spirit

working through preaching even when our experiences are less dramatic and stand out less?
2. What implications does preaching in demonstration of the Spirit and of power have for the content and manner of preaching? Does outward form matter in preaching?
3. How can you foster the power of the Spirit in the preacher as well as in yourself as you listen to sermons?
4. Why is Christ tied so tightly to every aspect of Christian faith and life? How should this affect what we expect to receive in preaching?

4

WHAT ARE THE PROPER AIMS OF PREACHING?

> Him we preach, warning every man and teaching every man in all wisdom, that we may present every man perfect in Christ Jesus. To this *end* I also labor, striving according to His working which works in me mightily.
>
> — COLOSSIANS 1:28-29

We need to eat, drink, breathe, and sleep in order to live. Yet we also need God's sustaining grace in order to live. People sometimes respond in strange ways to the sovereign work of the Holy Spirit in the preached Word. Some reason that if the Spirit alone changes people's hearts, then it does not matter how well ministers reason with sinners or, in some cases, whether anyone preaches the gospel to them at all. This is like saying that since God can keep us alive without food, he will keep us alive whether or not we eat.[1] Dead souls result from the first way of thinking and dead bodies from the second. What

God can do in his providence is a poor guide for what we should do in light of his Word.[2]

Hearing the Lord Jesus Christ

We need to hear Christ in order to believe in him for salvation (Romans 10:14). Ordinarily we hear his voice through his ordained ambassadors as they preach the gospel in demonstration of the Spirit's power (Romans 10:15; 2 Corinthians 5:19-6:2; 1 Corinthians 2:5). Yet we can believe these things and still make fatal mistakes in regard to preaching.

In Colossians 1:28-29, Paul shows that preaching requires hard labor in order to achieve its ends. The high aims of preaching demand the heavy labors of preachers. This passage asserts that ministers must preach Christ wisely for the salvation of all hearers. This includes their sanctification as well as their justification. We learn from these truths how and why the lofty aims of preaching flow from its content and determine its manner. This reinforces previous chapters on these themes and expands them in relation to the aims of preaching.

The primary object of preaching

Ministers must preach Christ ("Him we preach" v. 28a). Why did Paul consistently treat Christ as the sum and substance of his preaching? Other passages surveyed in this book showed that Christ is the primary object of preaching because, through preaching, Christ brings sinners to the Father by the Spirit's power. Colossians 1 adds that Christ is the primary substance of preaching (v. 28) because Christ builds his church through ministers who suffer for his sake (v. 24-25), because he is the substance of the divine mystery that God has now revealed (v. 26-27), and because union with Christ is the "hope of glory" for believers (v. 27; Philippians 3:20-21).

Ministers embody Christ's ministry on behalf of the church. Christ is the reason for their sufferings, the content of their message, and the ground of their hopes. Why, then, must Christ be the sum and substance of their preaching? He must be so because ministers live in communion with Christ as they aim to bring others into communion with him, because they should be consumed with the divine mystery regarding him above all else, and because he must remain the center of their hope.

Christ is the bridge between preaching the glory of the Triune God and all other subjects in relation to God.[3] Preaching "the whole counsel of God" (Acts 20:27) without relating all things in it to Christ's person and work is like trying to view a beautiful landscape without the light of the sun. Is it "him we preach"? Is it him we want to hear about?

Preaching and wisdom

Ministers must preach Christ wisely ("in all wisdom" v. 28b). What does it mean to preach Christ? Negatively, preaching Christ is not merely describing Christ. What would we think of a man who described a woman clearly, accurately, and dispassionately only to learn later that the woman was his wife? Preaching is not like giving a physical description of a suspect to a detective. It is more like singing for joy over one whom our souls love (Song 3:1, 4). It is like the friend of the bridegroom waiting eagerly to introduce the bridegroom to his bride (John 3:29).

Positively, preaching Christ must be done "in all wisdom." Preaching Christ should be specific and direct ("warning every man"). The purposes of preaching reflect the purposes of Scripture. Wisdom for salvation through faith in Christ includes reproof and correction as well as doctrine and instruction in righteousness (1 Timothy 3:15-17). "Warning" entails application. "Warning every man" demands specific application. Preaching should be instructive as well ("teaching every man").

As Westminster Larger Catechism 159 states, "They that are called to labour in the ministry of the Word, are to preach sound doctrine, diligently, in season and out of season; plainly, not in the enticing words of man's wisdom, but in demonstration of the Spirit, and of power; faithfully, making known the whole counsel of God." Preaching must aim to convict individual hearers by applying the teachings of Scripture to them directly. Preachers must know the people to whom they preach. Refuting irrelevant errors that people do not face is like shooting without taking aim. Preachers should visit the people to whom they preach regularly in order to know them personally and the challenges they face.

Application should not be so specific that ministers betray trusts and embarrass people publicly in sermons, yet they should be specific enough to warn and teach "every man." In doing so, preachers preach "wisely, applying themselves to the necessities and capacities of their hearers" (WLC 159).

Preaching for salvation

Preachers must preach Christ for the salvation of all hearers (v. 28c). "Every man" appears three times in this passage. We cannot be content to leave anyone behind in preaching. We cannot adopt a "take it or leave it" mentality to the means of grace, in which we preach dull sermons and blame the Holy Spirit for the unbelief of our hearers.

Preaching should be zealous and passionate.[4] Preachers must preach "zealously, with fervent love to God and the souls of his people; sincerely, aiming at his glory, and their conversion, edification, and salvation" (WLC 159). Preaching should neither be boring nor harsh. The pulpit is not a platform for beat up pastors to lash back at difficult people. We must keep the final goal of salvation in view. God aims to present every man perfect in Christ, not merely to justify them. These things should shape our aims and expectations in listening to sermons as well.

Paul concludes that preaching is dependent labor ("striving according to His working, which works in me mightily"). Periodically, people would tell my wife how nice it must be that, as a pastor, her husband only had to work one day a week! She often shocked them by telling them that I usually worked roughly sixty hours a week. She explained how many people I visited, how much counseling and discipleship I did, how many meetings I had with my elders, my work on presbytery and denominational committees, etc. Yet the mystery remaining for them was the fact that I spent most of my time each week praying and studying for the preaching of the Word.

The world asks why anyone would devote their lives to studying one book in order to preach it to other people who paid them to do it every week, let alone why it should take so long to do it. Yet preaching aims to bring dead souls to life in Christ and to keep them alive by the Spirit. Labor demands that preachers spend a lot of time in the study. Dependent labor means that they must bathe all of their studies with prayer for themselves and for those who hear them. Ultimately, we should expect ministers of the Word to pray and to preach (Acts 6:4), and to work hard doing both.

The challenge

By now, readers should detect a pattern in biblical texts that describe preaching. Christ is the primary object of preaching. He reaches sinners by his Word and Spirit, using ministers as his instruments. He is the subject, object, and end of preaching. This pattern raises several questions for preachers. Do you preach to the glory of God in Christ? Doing so keeps your preaching on track. Do you preach Christ experimentally? Does Christ live in your affections in order to bring life to others through your sermons? This makes your preaching lively. Do you preach Christ pointedly?

Preaching without specific and pointed application violates the biblical definition of preaching just as much as failing to preach Christ does. Pointed preaching is part of what makes Spirit-filled preaching effective. Those who repeat Christ's story without pressing Christ on individual consciences and those who press people with duties without preaching Christ fail equally in the aims of preaching. Do you labor hard in preaching with the Spirit's help? This is what makes preaching powerful.

It is not enough to read Bible commentaries, though many preachers need to read more of them than they do. Commentaries help us understand the text, but they do not help us meet the goals of preaching. Though the Spirit is sovereign in his work, lacking zeal, vigor, or diligence in preaching is a better indicator of laziness than of faith. Preaching must be lively, convicting, instructive, specific, and laborious. Only such preaching can aim to present every man perfect in Christ.

The pattern set by these texts also raises questions for listeners. Do we desire pointed application in sermons? Do we seek the Spirit to sanctify us in Christ and help us persevere to glory as we sit under preaching? Do our hearts reflect the biblical aims of preaching and is this the kind of preaching that we want?

Study Questions

1. How does Colossians 1 stress the importance of Christ in the plan of God? Why does this have far reaching consequences for Christian preaching and Christian living?
2. What does it mean to preach Christ wisely? What implications does this have for how we respond to personal application in sermons?
3. How can we take sermons personally? In light of the personal aims of preaching, how can we learn to use sermons well even if the preacher does not address our particular needs directly?
4. How can we help preachers in their labors in preaching the Word?
5. How do the passages treated in the first four chapters of this book relate to preaching Christ? What does this teach us about the agenda that the Bible sets for preaching and for what we should expect in preaching?

5

WHAT ARE THE SPIRIT'S AIMS IN PREACHING?

And when He has come, He will convict the world of sin, and of righteousness, and of judgment: of sin, because they do not believe in Me; of righteousness, because I go to My Father and you see Me no more; of judgment, because the ruler of this world is judged...He will glorify Me, for He will take of what is Mine and declare *it* to you. All things that the Father has are Mine. Therefore, I said that He will take of Mine and declare *it* to you.

—JOHN 16:8-11, 14-15

The American Congress, parliaments, and presbyteries all have at least one thing in common: they use *Robert's Rules of Order* to direct their meetings. One of the basic rules in this system is that forward momentum always begins with a motion. Every motion needs a second; otherwise it dies. Preaching is like Christ making a motion on the Father's behalf through his ambassadors. The Spirit seconds Christ's motion in people's hearts, moving them to God in Christ.

We must define preaching biblically, know why it is necessary, preach and listen to sermons in the right way, and understand the aims of preaching. Yet our aims in relation to preaching must match the Spirit's aims in general. What we must do in preaching reflects what Christ sent the Spirit to do through preaching.

The convicting work of the Spirit

John 16:8-11, 14 shows that the Spirit aims to glorify Christ by convicting the world of sin, of righteousness, and of judgment. The material below will explain each part of this proposition in detail. Jesus here describes these aims both broadly and narrowly, together with the reasons standing behind them.

The Spirit aims generally to convict the world of sin, righteousness, and judgment (v. 8). The Spirit's aims, according to the Greek text of this verse, are "elenctic." This loan word from Greek means, "to refute," or, "to convict."[1] Conviction can mean different things in English. A convicted criminal may go to prison, get out, and end up being convicted of a fresh crime. Alternatively, a person of conviction is someone who sticks to their principles whatever the cost. John has in view something more like confronting someone's wrong beliefs and practices so convincingly that they are left without excuse.

Though preaching is not in view directly in this

passage, previous chapters have shown that the Lord convicts the world through preaching by way of "warning," "reproof," and "correction." In this regard, the Spirit's aims in preaching match his goals in giving us the Scriptures (2 Timothy 3:16-17). The Spirit aims to convict people. His work through sermons reflects this general aim. The Spirit's work is convicting because he produces repentance towards God and faith in Jesus Christ (Acts 20:21).

Sermons that do not aim at conviction are not truly Christian sermons to the extent that they do not share the Spirit's concerns. Do you desire and expect to be convicted under the preaching of the Word? Do you desire the Word to work in you like a sharp two-edged sword that judges the thoughts and intents of your heart (Hebrews 4:12)? The Great Physician wounds us through his Word and Spirit before he heals us by the same Word and Spirit.

The centrality of the Lord Jesus Christ

The Spirit aims specifically to convict the world of sin, righteousness, and judgment in relation to Christ. It is easy to misconstrue Christ's words to fit our preconceived ideas. He did not say "of sin" because they have broken the Ten Commandments, "of righteousness" because they need Christ's imputed righteousness, and "of judgment" because the Day of Judgment is coming. While Christ says that about the Spirit "He will glorify Me" (v. 14), do we not tend to say instead, "it is all about me?"

The popular way of understanding this text sketched above is that the Spirit's work is primarily about my sin, rather than my sin in relation to Christ; about the righteousness that I need, rather than the fact that Christ is the Righteous One; and about the judgment that I face rather than the judgment that Christ brought. Even in our justified quest for application in sermons, we can develop subtly selfish expectations that make ourselves the primary object of the Spirit's work rather than Christ. In order to appreciate this fact better, it is important to examine each of the three activities of the Spirit listed in these verses in turn.

Though we should define sin in terms of breaking God's law (1 John 3:4), some sins are worse in God's sight than others. It will be more tolerable for Sodom on the Day of Judgment than for those who reject the gospel of Christ (Matthew 11:24). Sins against the gospel are weightier than sins against the law (Hebrews 2:1-4), since rejecting God's mercies in Christ tarnishes the honor of every divine attribute and of all three divine persons. "Righteousness" refers to Christ's vindication by the Father. His resurrection constituted his "justification" in the Spirit (1 Timothy 3:16), because death was for sinners and not for a righteous man (Acts 2:24; Romans 6:23).

The Spirit convicts people that righteousness belongs to the Lord while "shame of face" belongs to them (Daniel 9:7). God vindicates believers through Christ's imputed righteousness because he first vindicated Christ in his inherent righteousness. In Jesus Christ, the Righteous One, we have righteousness and strength (1 John 2:1;

Isaiah 45:24). "Judgment" means that "the ruler of this world," namely Satan, (John 12:31; 2 Corinthians 4:4) has come under judgment already. Through Christ's death, he "destroyed" the devil, "who had power over death" (Hebrews 2:14). Christ has "bound" the strong man and he is plundering his goods by saving the nations (Mark 3:27; Revelation 20:1-3).

Christ has defeated sin, death, and Satan. The Spirit convicts people that he who sins is a slave of sin (John 8:34), that Christ brings sinners from death to life (1 John 3:14), and that he translates them out of the kingdom of darkness into the kingdom of the Son of his love (Colossians 1:13).

Preaching should be convicting, but a sermon is not a good sermon simply because it is convicting. Christ defined the Spirit's convicting work in relation to himself. Conviction is a vital part of preaching, but conviction can never be the final goal of preaching. Preaching should convict us in relation to Christ and conviction under preaching must lead us towards Christ.

Glorifying Christ

The next part of the text explains the Spirit's Christ-centered aims. The reason why the Spirit aims to glorify Christ, in preaching and in everything he does in our lives, relates to the Spirit's relation to the Father and the Son. The Triune God does what he does in time because he is who he is in eternity. The Father begets the Son from eternity and the Spirit proceeds from the Father and the

Son. Christ received his words and works from the Father (John 14:10) because he is eternally begotten of the Father. As the Spirit proceeds from the Father and the Son eternally, so the "Spirit of truth" would guide his disciples into "all truth." He declared to the disciples what he received from the Son (John 16:12-14). The Spirit reveals and applies Christ's will even as Christ proclaimed and fulfilled the Father's will (v. 15).

The persons of the Trinity work according to the order in which they subsist in the Godhead. The Spirit has no personal subsistence apart from the Son and the Spirit always brings people to the Father through the Son. This is why the summary aim of the Spirit's work is to glorify Christ ("He shall glorify Me," v. 14).

These things may be a great mystery, but without them we cannot understand how we relate to all three persons in the Trinity under the gospel. These truths are not fully comprehensible to our minds, but they can be apprehended by faith. Preaching must aim to glorify Christ in every sermon in order to match the Spirit's aims in preaching.

Likewise, we must lay hold of our glorious Savior in every aspect of what he wants us to believe and do from the beginning of the Christian life to its end. Christ-centered preaching merely reflects the person of the Christ-centered Spirit, to the glory of the Father.

Driving people to Christ

Preachers must preach sermons that the Spirit can second. Christ is "moved" in the sermon. Without the motion and the Sprit's "second," the sermon dies in the mouth of the preacher and in the ears of the hearers. Preaching is inherently confrontational. Spirit-filled preaching must confront people in order to drive them to Christ.

I have heard pastors complain frequently of people leaving churches because they preach the law of God. All who preach the law will face this sad reality. This relates to my comments on the positive content of preaching noted in a previous chapter. We must remember that not all law-preaching aims high enough. Do we preach the law of God as culminating in sin against Christ, as fulfilled by Christ, as directing all people to Christ, and as rewritten on our hearts in Christ? Spirit-filled preaching must respect the order of operations in the Trinity as well, which will be the subject of the next chapter.

How should we respond to these truths as hearers? We should not erect barriers against the Spirit's convicting work through sermons. We should welcome the Spirit's work of conviction. We should acknowledge our sin and unbelief as we sit under the Word rather than try to excuse them. We should come to sermons to hear of Christ and not merely to solve our problems. We should recognize the Spirit's ministry to us through preaching and we should welcome rather than resist his work.[2]

Study Questions

1. What does it mean for the Spirit to convict the world? In what ways has the Spirit convicted you in the preaching of the Word when you were not expecting it?
2. How can we submit to the Spirit's convicting work through preaching? What should be our attitude when we disagree with the pastor at points in his sermon? Is it possible that the Spirit is still aiming to convict us through these things?
3. Give examples of how we sometimes unintentionally make the Spirit's convicting work about ourselves rather than about Christ?
4. Why is the doctrine of the Trinity important for understanding how the Spirit works in the Christian life?
5. How does the Spirit's work though preaching relate to the way in which he works in every other aspect of the Christian life? Give some examples.

6

HOW DOES PREACHING RELATE TO THE MISSIONS OF THE PERSONS OF THE TRINITY?

Jesus said to her, "Woman, believe Me, the hour is coming when you will neither on this mountain, nor in Jerusalem, worship the Father. You worship what you do not know; we know what we worship, for salvation is of the Jews. But the hour is coming, and now is, when the true worshipers will worship the Father in spirit and truth; for the Father is seeking such to worship Him. God *is* Spirit, and those who worship Him must worship in spirit and truth.

—John 4:21-24

Seeking the lost

What would happen if your child were lost in the woods? What would you do to find him or her? You would retrace your steps, using every tool at your disposal to find them. You would call the police. You would send out a search party. You would gather your neighbors, friends, and family to help you look. You would put out notice for others to help. Yet, all of these people would be seeking for your lost child for one simple reason: you were seeking the child first and you enlisted their help. If you had not told them that the child was missing, then they would not have known to look. If they find the child, then it is because you took the initiative and got the search going.

Similarly, preaching seeks out the Father's lost and wandering sheep because the Father himself is seeking them. Where the analogy breaks down is that the Triune God is able to call sinners to himself without us. He both calls and brings people to himself (John 6:44, 65). He chooses to use human instruments when he does not need them. Standing behind the preaching of the Word is a Father who calls his elect into his family, a Son who incorporates them into his body, and a Spirit who makes them living stones in his temple.

Every divine work reflects God's Triunity. This means that if we want to understand what God is doing in our lives we must begin with who God is the Father always acts through his Son and by his Spirit. We come to the Father, by the Spirit, through the Son (Ephesians 2:18). Preaching in relation to other biblical topics is like the relationship of countries to continents and continents to the world. Preaching must fit into the broader picture of the plan and work of the Triune God.

John 4:21-24 gives insight into the theological world in which preaching is found by describing the goal of evangelism. Since the Father is seeking people to worship him in Spirit and in truth, preaching should aim to produce people who worship the Father by the Spirit through the Son. Relating preaching to the work of the Trinity is important because it ties together what preaching is, its necessity, its manner, and its aims in light of the doctrine of God, which is the center of the theological universe of Scripture.[1]

First, the Father is seeking worshipers (v. 23). Many people are hopeless today because they have no sense of purpose in their lives. We will remain hopeless as long as we believe that the big question of "the meaning of life" is unanswerable. Worship is the primary purpose of life and worship is the primary context of this passage in John. The Father gives us hope by seeking to acknowledge that he is on the throne and that we exist for him and not for ourselves. Jews and Samaritans had no dealings with one another (v. 9) because they disagreed sharply over how to worship God.

Jesus promised to give the woman of Samaria living water that would satisfy her thirsty soul, giving her eternal life (v. 10-14). When she wanted this water, Jesus confronted her with the fact that she had had five husbands (v. 15-18). By this, the woman knew that Jesus was a prophet (v. 19). As such, he was suited to teach her how to worship the Father. As they stood at the foot of the place of Samaritan worship, which embodied the Jewish/Samaritan division, she went to the heart of the matter by asking Jesus where the proper place of worship was (v. 20). She was not changing the subject. Jesus responded that her question would become irrelevant because all people would soon worship the Father in every place rather than on one mountain (v. 21). The second thing that he said was that Jewish worship was right and Samaritan worship was wrong (v. 22).

Worship belonged to the Jews because salvation belonged to the Jews. To them were committed "the oracles of God" (Romans 3:2). In God's light we see light (Psalm 36:9), but worship that is not informed by Scripture lies under the darkness of ignorance. The Father is seeking worshipers. Salvation is the means to this end. This is an encouraging thought! It means that the Father is more willing to offer us life in the gospel than we often are to receive it. Preaching must match the Father's missionary aim. Christ himself pursued this aim as he brought the gospel to this woman.

Second, the Father is seeking worshipers in Spirit. I am from California. Sometimes I think that Californian culture and customs are in my DNA. Yet I would likely feel differently if I grew up elsewhere. The Father is seeking worshipers whose identities go much deeper than their cultural backgrounds and upbringing. He is seeking worshipers whose spiritual DNA is fundamentally altered by the indwelling presence of the Holy Spirit. Yet Jesus uses the term "Spirit" in two different ways in this passage.

First, because "God is Spirit" (v. 24), he is not confined to temples (1 Kings 8:21; 2 Chronicles 2:6; 6:18). Like the earth we stand on and the air we breath, he is there wherever we go. He is also there where we can't live and breath, and even beyond. He is immense. Since he gives life and breath to all things, he cannot be served with the works of men's hands (Acts 17:25). God's spiritual essence extends beyond Jerusalem and Judea to Samaria and to the uttermost parts of the earth (Acts 1:8). The Old Testament movement in toward Jerusalem has become a movement out from Jerusalem, bringing the gospel to the rest of the world.

Second, the God who is Spirit seeks worshipers through the person and work of the Holy Spirit (John 4:23-24). We must worship the Father in the Spirit, both because we must be born of water and Spirit if we would see the kingdom of God (John 3:5), and because the Spirit takes what belongs to Christ and reveals it to us (John 14:15). As the Son does what he sees the Father do, and the Father reveals all that he has to the Son, so the Father gives sinners life through the Son and has committed all judgment to the Son (John 5:19-23). The Holy Spirit regenerates us so that we can believe in Christ and worship the Father with sincere hearts and unhypocritical faith. Preaching in the Spirit's power aims to produce worshipers in Spirit.

Third, the Father is seeking worshipers in truth (John 4:23-24). This means that we must worship the Father in and through Christ. Worshiping in Spirit is like raising a corpse and infusing with a new living principle more powerful and effective than any life that person knew before. Worshiping in truth is like living in a new home, walking on a new path, becoming one flesh with a spouse, being a member of a body, and many more things all at once. Being united to Christ and knowing the Father through him is indescribably necessary and incomprehensibly glorious.

The law came through Moses, but grace and truth came through Jesus Christ (John 1:17). No one has seen God at any time, but Christ, who is the only begotten Son dwelling in the bosom of the Father, reveals the Father to us (John 1:18). Christ teaches the truth that sets people free from slavery to sin (John 8:32). Christ is the way, the truth, and the life and no one comes to the Father except through him (John 14:6). Christ would send the Spirit to lead his followers into all truth (John 16:13). He would do so by glorifying Christ (v. 14). Christ's continues to do these things in the church today through his Word and Spirit (Isaiah 59:20-21). Preaching should always reflect that fact that the Father seeks worshipers through and in his Son.

Trinitarian preaching

The missions of the divine persons remind us that preaching must be God-centered. The Father is the great parent who is not merely seeking his lost children. He makes them children by adopting them in his Son as he puts his Spirit in them. This sets the tone for the entire Christian life, both as individuals and as the church. It also sets the tone for evangelism and for preaching. All evangelism should be doxological and all doxology should be evangelistic. Like the Psalmist, our souls should boast in the Lord and we should call others to magnify the Lord with us (Psalm 34:2-3).

Preaching must respect the processions and missions of the divine persons.[2] The gospel is trinitarian because what God does reflects who God is (Ephesians 1:3-14). As Reeves notes, "Preaching is a natural expression of this God's identity. The Spirit who speaks what he has heard enables preachers to join in with God's own proclamation of his Son. To preach Christ is to participate in the life of God."[3]

Preaching must reflect the missionary goal of the Father. Do we seek worshipers through preaching sermons and do we seek to worship when hearing them?

Preaching must promote dependence on the Spirit to produce sincere worshipers. Do we acknowledge the necessity of the Spirit's inward work in us in preaching and hearing sermons?

Preaching must aim to bring people to worship the Father through Christ, who reveals himself in Scripture. Do we preach Christ from Scripture and worship God in light of Scripture? Do we come to sermons expecting to worship the Father in Spirit and in truth? Such questions should shape how we hear sermons and how ministers preach them. The purposes of worship and of preaching are to honor the Father and then to promote our edification. Sermons are for God more than they are for us, and the Triune God works through sermons to put God in his proper place and us in ours.

Study Questions

1. How is the doctrine of the Trinity relevant to evangelism? To the Christian life?
2. In what ways should the missions of the persons of the Trinity shape the content and goals of preaching?
3. Why should we expect the Father to seek worshipers through his Son and by his Spirit in preaching preeminently?
4. What does it mean to worship God in Spirit? What implications does worshiping in Spirit hold for our hearts and affections in worship?
5. What does it mean to worship God in truth? How does worshiping God in truth affect the way in which we approach God in worship?

7

WHAT ARE THE PROPER METHODS FOR PREACHING CHRIST? (1)

Owning a home brings blessings and liabilities with it. While a home can be a good investment it requires maintenance. Homeowners generally have two options in maintaining their homes: they can hire someone to do the work, or they need to get the tools and learn the skills that they need to do it themselves. They need to know what work needs to be done and how to use the right tools at the right time to do the job at hand.

Preachers must develop many tools in order to preach Christ biblically and effectively. It is one thing to know what preachers should do and why they should do it. It is another thing to ask how they should preach. It is important for non-preachers to understand these things too, so that they can know what to expect in preaching, how to pray for their preachers, what questions to ask when calling new pastors, and to develop prayerful sympathy with preachers as they understand how difficult true preaching can be.

Methods for preaching

As we saw in a previous chapter, preaching is a public authoritative proclamation of the gospel, through Christ's ordained ambassadors, in which Christ pleads with sinners to be reconciled to God. Preachers and listeners alike need to understand how this general definition applies to preaching biblical texts. Methods for preaching Christ should include exegesis, redemptive history, systematic theology, and personal devotion.

Exegesis means to explain sentences in the Bible in their contexts and understanding what parts of the Bible mean. Redemptive history means that God is telling us a story in his Word about how Jesus saves sinners and that he made this story clearer and fuller as its plot unfolded in history and culminated in Jesus' coming. Systematic theology refers to understanding what the entire Bible teaches and how its teachings relate to each other. Personal devotion means that the more we love Jesus, the more we will want to talk about him.

This chapter gives examples of preaching Christ exegetically and redemptive-historically while those that follow complete the picture of the preacher's tools through systematic theology and personal devotion to Christ. This material expands our understanding of what preaching is by showing what it should look like in practice in more detail. This helps us know better what to look for in sermons and how to encourage preachers in their difficult work.

Preaching exegetically

Preachers should preach Christ exegetically. Exegesis refers to an explanation or critical interpretation of a text. In my last year of high school, my English teacher asked the class to read *Beowulf*. This resulted in a universal series of F's for every student on every weekly quiz on the book. Initially, threatening to drive him to despair, the teacher thought that he had a particularly lazy class. However, when he began to read the book line by line in class, re-asking the quiz questions, he quickly realized something that he did not know before. The problem was not that the students were not reading the book, but that they barely understood a single line in it. When the teacher began to explain the story line by line, then they got it and even became excited about the story.

This is similar to what preachers must do in exegeting biblical texts. John 1:18 describes Christ as the one who exegetes the Father. As Christ interpreted and declared the Father to his hearers, so preachers must interpret and declare Christ to theirs. Christ said that the Scriptures testified to him (John 5:39).

Matthew's gospel proves repeatedly how Christ's person, actions, and work fulfilled Scripture. The risen Christ chided his disciples for not believing what the prophets said about Christ's sufferings and the glory that would follow, expounding what Moses and the prophets said about him (Luke 24:25:27). All Scripture is God-breathed and it is able to make people wise for salvation in Christ (1 Timothy 3:15) because all Scripture testifies ultimately to Christ. Exegesis is a direct means of preaching Christ because it pulls him out of the text right where he is and presents him to the congregation in three dimensions.

Christ and the Old Testament

Preachers must preach Christ exegetically from the Old Testament by explaining prophecies and promises about Christ. Christ is the path running straight through the OT, even though sometimes we are like those walking in the dark who can't always see the path before us clearly. He is the Seed of the Woman who crushed the serpent's head (Genesis 3:15). He is Abraham's seed in whom all the earth would be blessed (Genesis 22:18; Galatians 3:16). He is the Prophet like Moses (Deuteronomy 18:5; Acts 3:22; 7:37). He is David's Son and David's Lord (Psalm 110:1; Matthew 22:45). He is the shoot from Jesse's root who would rule as King (Isaiah 11:2) as well as the "root out of dry ground" (Isaiah 53:2) who would obey and suffer as Priest (Acts 8:30-36). He is the Priest whom God crowned as King (Zechariah 3:8-10, 6:12-13; Hebrews 7).

Preaching Christ from the Old Testament exegetically means locating specific signposts that point to Christ directly and immediately from various passages of the Bible.

The New Testament view

Preachers must preach Christ exegetically from the New Testament as well. While this might seem obvious, it is important to remember how the New Testament reveals Christ. The New Testament is not only like walking the same path laid in the Old Testament in the full noonday sun. It enables us to look back and see the road already travelled more clearly as well. The gospels reveal Christ's person and work through theologically charged history. The rest of the New Testament explains, expands, and applies the truths that the gospels reveal about Christ. The New Testament also provides the interpretive grid for finding Christ in the Old Testament. Its authors used the Scriptures in a way that focuses on Christ and they teach us how to do so.

Relating every text to Christ

Preachers should preach Christ in light of redemptive history as well. Redemptive history reflects the fact that the Bible has a main point in light of which the biblical story unfolds. If the Bible did not steadily tell a story of redemptive history, then there would be no exegetical signposts along the way to keep us on the right path. Preaching Christ redemptive-historically relates every text to Christ insofar as Christ's person and work are the main point of the teaching of the Bible as a whole.

This makes Christ relevant to every passage and every part of Scripture, even where it is not immediately obvious where we should see him in the text at hand. Sometimes we don't see him in the text of Scripture as much as we see him in the story of Scripture. To give a broad example, Genesis 3:15 serves as a thesis statement for the Bible's story-line by pitting Christ against Satan and Christ's people against Satan's people. A thesis statement is a one-line summary of everything that an author wants to say.

The sacrificial system both before and under Moses explains how Christ would gain victory for his people over sin, death, and Satan. The Exodus becomes a paradigm for redemption in Christ. The genealogies in 1 Chronicles show the progress of redemptive history up to that stage. Through redemptive history, we should learn to understand the parts of Scripture in light of the direction that the whole of Scripture is taking us.

The place of typology

Typology falls under the category of preaching Christ redemptive-historically as well. A type is a kind of picture that foreshadows something else. In a similar way, an engineer might construct a model or prototype of his planned product before he sends his plans to the assembly line. A biblical type may be an idea or a person. The temple is a type of Christ's body, through which God dwelt among his people (John 2:21). Adam is a type of Christ in his representative character (Romans 5:14). Melchizedek is a type of Christ's eternal priesthood (Hebrews 7). Types move the Bible's story forward by hinting at later and greater realities through earlier and lesser ones (Colossians 2:17). For example, every prophet, priest, and king in the Old Testament should direct us to Jesus as the final Prophet, Priest, and King in the New Testament.

Types do not correspond to their antitypes (or realities) in every respect. Sometimes Christ as antitype excels all types superlatively and sometimes he does so by contrast. Solomon was a type of Christ in both ways. Christ infinitely excelled Solomon's wisdom, prosperity, power, and borders without having any of his weaknesses. Preaching should include redemptive history and typology to help hearers relate particular passages of Scripture to the broader biblical storyline. Redemptive history reminds us that the biblical narrative is always going somewhere and that it always has an ultimately point that matters ultimately.

Using tools together

Exegesis and redemptive history are tools that help us understand Scripture in relation to Christ. Preaching Christ exegetically will eventually touch every aspect of Christ's person and work as well as the Spirit's work in applying his benefits to us through a regular course of preaching. Yet it will take a long time to do this and the results will often be a disjointed and irregular view of Christ and the gospel.

Preaching Christ redemptive-historically is more general in scope. It illustrates how Christ's place in God's plan creates the biblical narrative and gives significance to its parts.[1] However, if we isolate redemptive-historical preaching from other biblical tools for preaching Christ, then it runs the risk of telling a story that believers are not directly part of.

Knowing Christ (and preaching Christ) involves more than imagining that we are somehow characters in Christ's story. It involves actual participation in Christ, which comes only through knowing him personally by faith. The Bible refers to this as being "in Christ" or being united to Christ. Exegesis needs redemptive history just as redemptive history needs exegesis, but both need something more. Preaching Christ exegetically alone effectively removes Christ from most of the Old Testament. Exegesis without redemptive history is like reading road signs without knowing where the road is taking us. However, if preachers limit their methods for preaching Christ to exegesis and redemptive history, then they will still fall short at points of the biblical definitions and aims of preaching established in the first four chapters of this book.

Why are these things important as we listen to sermons? Among other things, they help us better grasp what the preacher is trying to do. In doing so, he is indirectly teaching us how to read our Bibles better as well. We should learn from sermons how to relate Scripture to Christ in our private Bible reading. Exegetical and redemptive-historical principles give us tools by which to evaluate what we hear as well. Though we should not adopt a critical spirit in listening to sermons, knowing how the Scriptures relate to Christ will help us profit from sermons more fully and learn how to grow in our love for Christ as we read and listen to his Word.[2]

∼

Study Questions

1. What is exegesis? What does it mean to preach Christ exegetically?
2. How can we learn to interpret the Bible well as we listen to sermons? Can you give examples where the Lord has used sermons to help you understand the Bible better?
3. How does redemptive history help us read and preach the Bible? How does this relate to the place of the gospel in Scripture?
4. What is typology? How is typology useful? Give some examples of where typology has been misused or abused.
5. Are exegesis and redemptive history useful tools for private Bible reading? How can we learn to apply these tools without putting too much pressure on ourselves to prepare our own messages on books and chapters of Scripture?

8

WHAT ARE THE PROPER METHODS FOR PREACHING CHRIST? (2)

If someone studies to be a medical doctor, then they must take one step at a time. They must enrol for the right classes in the right order. They must memorize information and pass exams. When the time comes, they must take a residency to study and practice their trade under other doctors. Yet what if someone took the right courses in the right order and memorized all of the information in every class, but did not learn the skills to connect the right pieces of information to a real patient sitting in their office? Going back to the chronological order of their courses and remembering when and where they learned about a particular disease or medicine will not be enough. Neither will simply knowing what medicines treat which symptoms be enough if they do not know how to think systematically and diagnose the disease and its root cause.

A good doctor does not simply revert to medical school or to a list of problems, but he or she learns how to bring the right information to bear on the right problems at the right times. A great doctor, however, is not only skilled at what they do but they love what they do. He or she walks the orderly path required through school, he or she learns to exegete the information gathered there, he or she systematizes the information needed and knows how to use it, and he or she works hard because they love both their profession and their patients.

Defining preaching by its aims

The case is similar with respect to great preaching. Sound exegesis, or explaining the words and grammar of passages of Scripture, is insufficient for sound preaching. Saying so might seem surprising in light of the popular resurgence of what people call consecutive expository preaching. This means preaching verse-by-verse through books of the Bible. While we should welcome and encourage the shift toward this kind of preaching due to its emphasis on biblical texts and books, it is not included in the Scriptural agenda set for preaching that we have seen in previous chapters.

The Bible defines preaching in terms of what it is and what its goals are. Scripture defines preaching, preaching should explain and apply Scripture, and preaching should be filled with Scripture. While preaching should ordinarily move straight through books of the Bible, we should remember that this is a pragmatic conclusion more than it is a biblical mandate. Expository preaching is a means of preaching, but it is not the end of preaching. Though I say this cautiously, because I do not want to discourage consecutive expository preaching, neither is this method inherent to the biblical definition of preaching. Preaching is a public, authoritative declaration of the gospel, by ordained ambassadors of Christ, through whom Christ calls people to be reconciled to God.

Preaching like the New Testament

Most New Testament examples of preaching Christ are theological and devotional rather than exegetical and redemptive-historical. This means that the authors of the New Testament connected Jesus to biblical teachings and their practical uses more than to the grammar of verses and even sometimes to their place in God's unfolding story. This does not necessarily establish a pattern for which texts pastors should preach from week to week.

There are good reasons to help people understand the books of the Bible by preaching through them verse by verse and one at a time. Yet the New Testament model for preaching Christ gives us more tools to work with than simply turning sermons into running Bible commentaries.

We can imitate the apostolic use of specific passages while still preaching consecutively through biblical books. However, asking whether preaching should be grammatical-exegetical or redemptive-historical does not give us enough options. Explaining texts as well as their place in God's story are both necessary, yet both of them are inadequate and incomplete by themselves for fulfilling the biblical purposes of preaching.

Connecting Christ to biblical passages theologically

and devotionally are the remaining two methods by which preachers should preach Christ. This chapter treats the theological necessity of preaching Christ while the next one explains its devotional necessity. Understanding how these tools work in preaching Christ helps us better understand how to pray for pastors as they prepare sermons and what to expect from them as they preach sermons.

Preaching Christ is necessary theologically. This means that pastors need to draw conclusions from the Bible's teaching as a whole in order to preach its central message in relation to each of its parts. As theological ideas appear in texts of Scripture, those ideas are biblical means of bringing Christ into sermons without reading him into every biblical text. Some examples will make this point easier to understand.

Theology and Christology

Theology refers to the study of God for the purpose of knowing him. Christology refers to the study of Christ for the purpose of knowing God through him. All theology depends on Christology, and all Christology directs to the glory of the Triune God as its highest end. The Holy Spirit teaches us Christology in the Bible so that we can learn true theology.

Christ puts every divine attribute on display distinctly and all of them together. He is like a prism in which we see all of the colours of God's glory one by one and all at once. He is "the blessed and only Potentate, the King of kings and Lord of lords, who alone has immortality, dwelling in unapproachable light, whom no man has seen or can see, to whom *be* honour and everlasting power. Amen" (1 Timothy 6:15-16). His person and work make the glorious constellation of divine attributes shine forth in radiant splendour.[1]

Christ shows us how we relate to the other persons of the Trinity. He is the Father's agent of creation (John 1:3; Colossians 1:16). He is the Father's instrument of redemption (Ephesians 1:7-12). He poured out the Spirit from the Father to equip the church for his mission (Acts 2:33).

Any text presenting the authority and majesty of God should lead us to the Father, who represents the majesty of the whole Trinity. Any text convicting us of sin or requiring repentance directs us to Christ, who removes sin and who is the pattern of godliness. Any text requiring us to do or to believe something directs us to the Spirit, who illumines our minds and renews our hearts to believe and obey God. What passage of the Bible does not relate to these things? We cannot preach or worship one person of the Trinity without preaching or worshipping all three. The doctrine of God (theology) precedes the doctrine of Christ (Christology) in order of priority. Yet without Christology the doctrine of God by itself cannot fulfill the goals of preaching.

Our relation to God

The doctrine of salvation (soteriology) revolves around the doctrine of Christ (Christology). Every biblical text relates to soteriology in some way because all Scripture says something about our relation to God. Christ's person and work is the summary of the gospel (1 Timothy 3:16). His person is the ground of the gospel and we receive his benefits through union with him by faith. God justifies us by forgiving our sins and accepting us as righteous through Christ's death and resurrection (2 Corinthians 5:21; Romans 4:21). Christ was born of a woman and made under the law so that we might receive the Spirit of adoption (Galatians 4:4; Romans 8:15). Christ is the essential image of God because he is the eternal Son of God (Hebrews 1:3) who renews in us the created image of God because we are adopted sons of God (Ephesians 4:24; Colossians 3:10). He is our sanctification. This means both that he sets us apart to be his own holy people and that he makes us obey God in holiness by his Word and Spirit.

In Christ, we persevere to the end and enter into glory, or heaven. In summary, Paul wrote, "But of him you are in Christ Jesus, who has become for us wisdom from God – and righteousness and sanctification and redemption" (1 Corinthians 1:30). Every part of the Bible that says anything about any of these subjects requires ministers to appeal to Christ theologically as the summary of the gospel and as the only means of salvation.

Christ the Head

The doctrine of the church and of the last things is meaningless apart from Christ. He is the Head of the church, which is his body (1 Corinthians 12:27; Colossians 1:18). The sacraments of the church (Baptism and the Lord's Supper) point to our union with Christ and with his people. We are all baptized into one body (1 Corinthians 12:13). We are one bread and one body in the Lord (1 Corinthians 10:17). We cannot belong truly to the church without being united to Christ and we cannot be united to Christ without being united to his people. The sacraments embody and seal both realities to believers. A seal is a mark showing who owns something. The sacraments are marks that God owns believers.

At the last Day, Christ will judge the world in righteousness (Acts 17:31). Our bodily resurrection in Christ is the goal of our redemption (1 Corinthians 15). Our highest blessedness will consist in seeing Christ as he is and being made like him (1 John 3:1-2). Our hope in this blessed sight (beatific vision) is one of the primary reasons why we pursue holiness now (v. 3). As Charles McIlvaine wrote, "Ask the way to heaven, we say, *Christ*. Ask where heaven is, we say, *where Christ is*. Ask what heaven is, we answer, *what Christ is*."[2] Any biblical passage that relates to the church, the sacraments, and the last things gives ministers means by which to preach Christ and, in so doing, to fulfill the goals of preaching.

Preaching Christ theologically shows that pastors need more than commentaries to prepare sermons. Preachers should not drive their sermons off their exegetical rails by turning sermons into theological lectures, even if they are practical lectures. Preaching straight through books of the Bible helps hearers understand the

Bible as a whole better. Doing so helps offset the biases and imperfections of ministers by preventing them from preaching their favourite texts and topics only. Yet God's designs in preaching are rarely met through the relatively straightforward process of exegetical labours. We must use many tools to preach Christ.

Preaching Christ is part of the biblical definition of preaching; preaching redemptive or grammatical-historical sermons is not enough by itself. Without undermining the value of these kinds of sermons, we should remember that the purpose of explaining texts in their contexts is to preach Christ from those texts. Making exegesis an end in itself in preaching is like learning to be an expert bricklayer in order to lay bricks instead of constructing walls or buildings. Making theological connections is just as necessary to preach biblically as is exegesis and biblical theology. Several subsequent chapters will illustrate what this looks like in practice.

Why is it important for hearers of sermons to be aware of theological connections made in preaching? The importance of theology, for those hearing sermons, has to do with the structure of the human mind and the nature of truth as God revealed it. God commands us to love him with our whole mind (Matthew 22:37; Mark 12:30; Luke 10:27). Doing so requires systematic ordering and arranging material and drawing conclusions from it. Christ expected the Sadducees to understand this fact (Mark 12:24-27) and he rebuked them for not doing so.

Knowing systematic theology in some measure enriches the Christian life. This is comparable to the pleasure one derives when listening to a symphony and being able to recognize the main theme and to see how the composer weaves that theme in and out of his piece. Knowing some systematic theology will give you a road map so that you and the preacher can stay on the same page in light of Scripture.[3]

∽

Study Questions

1. Why is the theology of the Bible as a whole in its interconnected parts so important to sound preaching? How does preaching Christ relate to preaching the whole counsel of God?
2. Why does theology make Christ relevant to any text or topic of Scripture? How would this relate to a topic like hospitality or ministering to widows?
3. Why are Christology and eschatology tied together so integrally? What effect should thinking about the last things have on the Christian life and on preaching?
4. In what ways did Christ expect his hearers to make broader theological connections in Scripture? What are some means that we can use to understand the theology of the Bible as a whole better?

9

WHAT ARE THE PROPER METHODS FOR PREACHING CHRIST? (3)

When a man and a woman are engaged to be married they can hardly talk about anything else. In fact, we might suspect that something is wrong if they don't express excitement about the wedding. The church is espoused to Christ and looks forward to the marriage supper of the Lamb (Revelation 19:6-9). Christ's love compelled Paul's preaching (2 Corinthians 5:14) and he denounced himself with maledictions if he failed to preach the gospel (1 Corinthians 9:16). In the end, ministers must preach Christ because they want to preach Christ. Christ should be central to their sermons because both preachers and listeners cannot bear to be without him whom their souls love (Song of Solomon 3:1).

More heart than method

This chapter is the third and final one treating the proper methods of preaching Christ. It shows that preaching

Christ is more a matter of the heart than the application of method. Preaching Christ is not ultimately a technique. Preaching Christ is a devotionally necessary response to the preacher's relation to Christ. As Sinclair Ferguson wrote, "preaching Christ must become instinctive, not formulaic."[1] Paul summarized the aims of the gospel in terms of preaching "repentance toward God and faith toward our Lord Jesus Christ" (Acts 20:21). The nature of saving faith and repentance, through which we exercise hope and love, highlights the reasons behind this devotional necessity.

The nature of saving faith makes preaching Christ necessary devotionally. While saving faith receives the whole Word of God because it is God's Word, "the principal acts of saving faith are accepting, receiving, and resting upon Christ alone for justification, sanctification, and eternal life, by virtue of the covenant of grace" (WCF 14.2). John Calvin noted that all acts of saving faith should take us to Christ, "For God would have remained hidden afar off if Christ's splendor had not beamed upon us."[2] Christ is the pioneer and the perfector of our faith (Hebrews 12:2). Faith involves being confident that God is able to perform whatever he promises (Romans 4:21). Christ is both the example and object of faith for believers.

Without faith it is impossible to please God (Hebrews 11:6). Faith trusts that if we pray according to God's will he hears us (1 John 5:14-15). Faith teaches us to pray in Christ's name (John 14:13-14), asking mercy from God for his sake and "drawing our encouragement to pray, and our boldness, strength, and hope of acceptance in prayer, from Christ and his mediation" (WLC 180). Ministers preach hoping that those hearing them will either come to faith in Christ or that they will grow in their faith in Christ (Ephesians 4:13). Their own faith in Christ and their desire to foster saving faith in others must always lead them to preach Christ as the object of faith.

True repentance

The nature of repentance unto life makes preaching Christ necessary devotionally. Repentance requires a true sense of sin in relation to its nature and not merely out of fear to its consequences. Sin is not hateful primarily because it is dangerous to sinners, but because it is offensive to God. We saw in a previous chapter from John 16:8-11 the relationship between Christ and the conviction of sin. Repentance involves grief and hatred for sin and turning from sin to God.

Not all sorrow for sin is godly sorrow and not all sorrow for sin leads to life instead of to death (2 Corinthians 7:10). Some people, like Peter, hate sin in its nature because they love Christ. Other people, like Judas, hate sin in its effects because they got caught. Remorse for sin is not repentance from sin. Before purposing and endeavoring after new obedience, we must apprehend God's mercies in Christ (WSC 87). Repentance creates a cycle or a tug of war between indwelling sin on the one side and increasing holiness on the other. Faith in Christ alone gives forward momentum to repentance.

The essential centrality of the Lord Jesus Christ

It speaks volumes about the state of Christianity at the present day that preachers and hearers need to be told that preaching Christ should be central in preaching. When I travel with my wife, I often overhear her speaking to strangers because I hear my name almost rhythmically. She and I cannot refer to our lives together without referring to each other, and we don't want to. We love each other and we share life together and we can't help referring to each other. No one ever tells us to do this and if we ever stop doing it then something will have gone radically wrong with our marriage.

So it should be with preaching Christ and with desiring to want to hear him in sermons. Ferguson notes, "Of course we need to work with general principles as we develop as preachers; but it is a far greater desideratum that we develop an instinctive mindset and, corresponding to that, such a passion for Jesus Christ himself that we find our way to him in a natural and realistic manner rather than a merely formulaic one."[3]

It is a tragedy, if not an absurdity, that some people actually argue that sermons do not need to be Christocentric. This is like a bride not only lacking vigor and excitement over her betrothed, but arguing why such things are not really an important part of marriage. A practical problem in this regard is that many pastors who love Christ struggle with how to preach him to small struggling congregations in which almost all listeners are professing Christians. The corrective to this apparent problem is to remember that how ministers should preach Christ to believing congregations is not radically different from how they should preach him to unconverted people. Preachers must always set Christ's glory and beauty before their hearers as the object of their faith and as the means of their repentance.

Devotion to Christ

The Christian life is not radically different than our first conversion, since we live by faith in the Son of God (Galatians 2:20). If we live the entire Christian life through faith and repentance, then we must live the entire Christian life out of devotion to Christ. Preaching void of Christ cannot call hearers to faith and repentance in Christ. If preaching cannot call sinners to faith and repentance, then it cannot call them to do anything. If preachers preach Christ from devotional necessity, then the other methods of preaching Christ will fall into place more easily. Their pent-up joy and excitement over Christ will look for outlets.

We must love Christ more fervently if we would preach him more effectively. We must treasure Christ more greatly if we would hear Christ in the preached Word more expectantly. The pastor's devotion to Christ will make preaching Christ inescapable for him. Our devotion to Christ should make hearing Christ irresistible to us.

How should we respond to these things? Do we pray

for ourselves and for those who preach the gospel to us that the Spirit would so enflame their love for Christ that they cannot keep quiet about him? Do we pray daily in our private prayer that we would want to hear Christ and that our preachers would want to preach Christ? Do we carry this burden into daily family worship, asking the Spirit, who is the fountain of living waters, to cultivate our thirst for Christ that he should satisfy our thirst in the preaching of the gospel? Do we pray at the weekly church prayer meeting that the Spirit would captivate the pastor in his study and that he would prepare his people to hear Christ's voice in preaching and to bring those who either don't want to hear his voice or don't know what it sounds like?

Let those who preach Christ preach devotionally and let those who hear preaching pursue Christ devotionally, for themselves and for their preachers on their knees in prayer.

∽

Study Questions

1. What does it mean to preach Christ devotionally? Why does Christian devotion demand preaching Christ? How should preaching Christ flow naturally from Christian devotion?
2. How can we foster our devotion to Christ?

How should this affect our daily walks with the Lord?

3. Why do the nature of true faith and repentance foster devotion to Christ? Why does this set the tone for everything that we do in the Christian life?

4. How is the Christian life integrally related to our first conversion? Why should Christology never be treated as one of the basics of the Christian life that we move on from to bigger and better things?

5. What are some practical ways that we neglect devotion to Christ as we talk about various doctrines and practices? What are some ways that we can fix this problem?

10

WHAT SHOULD PREACHING CHRIST LOOK LIKE?

As children learn by watching their parents, so preachers and hearers learn much by looking at the apostles. The principles taught in the preceding nine chapters risk resembling a shapeless cloud instead of a face reflected in a mirror without adding concrete examples. This section provides an example of how Paul preached Christ while the next one applies these examples to preaching other passages of Scripture.

Preachers should imitate Paul in filtering the whole counsel of God through the person and work of Christ. Paul's first letter to the Corinthians illustrates how to do so. Though this book is an epistle and not a sermon, the range of issues treated in it provides great insight into Paul's teaching and ministry. This furnishes us with a plethora of examples for connecting Christ to virtually any biblical doctrine or practice.

Christ and his people

Paul grounded this epistle in the relationship between Christ and the saints (1 Corinthians 1:1-9). The church belongs to God and it is set apart to God in Christ (v. 2). The Corinthians called upon Christ as Lord together with all believers in every place (v. 2). Grace and peace came to them from the Father and the Son (v. 3). The church received graces and gifts from Christ (v. 4-7). In his faithfulness, God would preserve the saints in Christ to the end by virtue of their fellowship with him (v. 8-9). This introduction mirrors the nature and ends of preaching through its effects in believers' lives.

Paul confronted disunity in the church in light of the church's relation to Christ (chapters 1-4). Instead of dividing over who baptized them (1:10-14), the Corinthians should rally around Christ's cross (v. 17). Believers must stop thinking like worldly people by remembering that God's wisdom in Christ saves and unites them. By contrast, the world is united in treating Christ's gospel as foolishness (1:18-29).

Christ's all-sufficiency reminds believers that they must boast in God and not in men (1:30-31). In order to flee division, they must remember that Christ is the heart of the gospel message (2:1-5) and that the Spirit directs them to Christ by divine revelation (2:6-10) and illumination (2:11-16). Christians should not divide over their ministers (3:1-15), but they should look to their common foundation in Christ (3:11). The church as a whole is the temple of the Holy Spirit as well (3:16-17). Therefore, boasting in men reflects worldly wisdom rather than God's wisdom in Christ (3:18-23). Ministers are merely "stewards of the mysteries of God" (4:1) and believers must regard them as such (4:2-6).

Ministers, and being baptized by them, are not proper objects of boasting, since believers have all things through Christ alone (4:7-13). While believers should be thankful for their ministers, they must repent of their worldly thinking by remembering the conduct of their ministers in Christ (4:14-21). Christ is the ground of church unity and fellowship with Christ is the remedy for its disunity.

Church discipline

Paul connected church discipline and lawsuits to union with Christ (5:1-6:11). The church must deliver unrepentant sinners to Satan (excommunication) in Christ's name and with his power (5:1-5). Christ ratifies the act of excommunication in heaven through his personal presence when even two or three are gathered in his name for that purpose (Matthew 18:18-20).

Believers must purge out the leaven of unrepentant sinners from their midst in light of their fellowship with Christ. He is their Passover and the one who sacrificed himself for them (5:6-8). These directions apply equally to those living in other unrepentant sins (5:9-13). As believers exclude unrepentant Christians from their fellowship, they must avoid going to law against one another before unbelievers because they were "washed," "sanctified," and "justified in the name of the Lord Jesus and by the Spirit of our God" (6:1-11). Union with Christ shapes church discipline and relationships in the church.

Union with Christ

Paul related our union with Christ to questions about sexual immorality, which led into questions about marriage (6:12-7:40). While sexual immorality is wrong inherently, it is doubly wrong for Christians (6:12-20). Their bodies are both members of Christ (6:15) and temples of the Holy Spirit (6:19). Believers must glorify God in body and spirit because Christ "bought" them (6:20). Though Paul did not bring Christ to bear directly in his treatment of marriage, as he did in Ephesians 5:22-33, his teaching on marriage flows from the truths established by the believer's relation to Christ in 6:12-20. Communion with Christ by the Spirit is the primary reason for sexual purity.

Food offered to idols

Paul treated the question of eating food offered to idols in relation to Christ's role in forming Christian conscience (chapters 8-10). The question treated in these chapters may seem foreign to us. The issue was whether or not believers should eat food that was offered to idols. Such food might be for sale in the marketplace and unbelievers might invite believers to share a meal in which they served this food. Paul answered that idols are nothing because God created all things through Christ (8:6). Some

Christians were slow to recognize this fact (8:7-8). Those who knew that idols were nothing may eat, but they must beware of leading those without this knowledge into eating because, in doing so, they would sin against Christ through misinformed consciences (8:9-13).

Apostolic example

In chapter nine, Paul enforced his teaching by personal example. He did not use all of his rights in Christ at all times so that he might preach the gospel of Christ more effectively. Chapter ten completes his argument by citing the Old Testament on the dangers of idolatry by relating the Old Testament saints to Christ (10:1-13). The Lord's Supper teaches that believers have communion with Christ and his church (10:14-17). Therefore, we cannot have fellowship with Christ and demonic idols (10:18-22). Even though all food is clean and lawful to eat, we must avoid leading others into idolatry by doing all things to God's glory (10:23-31). Believers should imitate Paul as he imitated Christ (11:1). Communion with Christ determines how we should treat fellow believers.

Christ and worship

In chapters eleven through fourteen, Paul incorporated Christ into questions about public worship. Women should wear head coverings in worship in light of God's authority in Christ (11:2-16). Christians must leave aside their divisions at the Lord's Supper, since they must discern Christ's body together at the table (11:17-34). Believers should exercise spiritual gifts for the benefit of others in light of their common Spirit-inspired confession that Christ is Lord (12:1-3) and in light of the common source of their gifts through the Spirit under God in Christ (12:4-11). They must do so as members together of Christ (12:27-31). They must exercise their gifts out of love to the brethren (chapter 13). Regardless of their individual gifts, they must exercise them to edify the church (14:12), which is Christ's body. They must do all things decently and in order because of their relation to God through Christ by the Spirit established in chapter twelve. Union and communion with Christ directs our conduct in public worship.

Chapter fifteen presents Christ as the capstone of sound doctrine. His death and resurrection summarizes the gospel message. Proclaiming these truths is the goal of preaching (15:1-11). The rest of the chapter explains why denying Christ's resurrection annihilates the gospel and affirming it lies at the heart our hope.

The last chapter of 1 Corinthians brings Paul's application of Christology to its final resolution. While the section on "the collection for the saints" (16:1-3) does not mention Christ directly, 2 Corinthians 8-9 motivates believers to give generously in light of God's indescribable gift of Christ to them. After passing on greetings, Paul concluded, "If anyone does not love the Lord Jesus Christ, let him be accursed. O Lord, come! The grace of our Lord Jesus Christ *be* with you. My love *be* with you all in Christ Jesus. Amen" (16:22-24). Christians must pursue sound doctrine and godly practices out of love for Christ and in light of his second coming.

Even though 1 Corinthians is not a sermon it exemplifies everything treated in previous chapters about preaching. Christology is the bridge between the doctrine of God and every area of theology and practice. We must aim for the glory of God in all that we believe and do, but we must remember that the incarnate Christ is the one through whom alone we glorify God. Paul related Christ to every Christian doctrine and practice in all his other epistles, as Peter, John, and Jude did in theirs.

Paul's preaching was a public, authoritative proclamation of the gospel that aimed to present every man perfect in Christ. He preached Christ exegetically, redemptive-historically, theologically, and practically. Preachers must learn to imitate him. Christian doctrine and life lose their moorings when they are detached from their relation to Christ. Christ makes doctrine saving and he makes Christian living possible.

∼

Study Questions

1. Why is 1 Corinthians such a useful model for preaching, even though it is not a sermon?
2. In what ways does Paul show us how to think about preaching Christ theologically and devotionally?

3. Give some examples of how Christ and him crucified is relevant for overcoming disunity in the church or for repenting of sexual immorality.
4. How and why do the sacraments (Baptism and the Lord's Supper) help us think about every aspect of Christian faith and life in terms of union and communion with Christ?
5. How and why does Christ both make doctrine saving and living the Christian life possible? What implications does this have for our struggles with particular indwelling sins?

11

IS PREACHING CHRIST ALWAYS INHERENT TO PREACHING?

Suppose that someone studied everything that they could about skateboarding. They could explain all of the parts of the skateboard and tell you which brands made the best products. They could explain what each trick was and how to learn it. They could even direct you to the best spots to go skateboarding and tell you which shoes and clothes to wear. Yet what if you found out that they had never stepped on a skateboard? Telling you how to do something and actually doing it are two very different things. Knowledge must combine with skill, muscle development, muscle memory, time, and practice. As hard as it is to explain how to do difficult tricks on a skateboard, it is a lot harder to learn to do it yourself.

So it is with preaching. It is one thing to have a sound theory of preaching. It is another thing to stand behind a pulpit twice a week and preach Christ in demonstration of the Spirit and of power. Theory can fall apart when we meet instances in which we are not sure how to apply the biblical model of preaching. This is true both when preaching biblical books that do not appear to match the Scriptural pattern of preaching and when consecutive exegetical preaching does not lend itself immediately to preaching Christ. Approaching such texts requires prayer, wisdom, practice, and more prayer.

We must understand the general duty of preaching Christ in relation to different genres of Scripture. One way to do this is to providing select examples of applying the apostolic model of preaching to specific texts. The first example below is taken from a general assessment of the Book of James; the subsequent examples taken from Psalm 1 and the Book of Amos provide more concrete details.

Preaching James in the light of all Scripture

The Book of James does not readily fit the pattern of preaching found in the rest of the New Testament. James wrote little about Christ theologically and practically, mentioning his name twice only. He referred to himself as a bondservant of Christ (James 1:1). He urged believers to be impartial because Christ is *"the Lord* of glory" in whom they believe (2:1). His teaching sometimes resembles Christ's teaching in the Sermon on the Mount (e.g., 4:11-17. See Matthew 7:1-5 and 6:25-34, respectively), but he does not mention Christ as the source, means, or aim of his teaching in these sections. Reading James is like reading a New Testament version of the Book of Proverbs. James shows us that not all New Testament authors emphasized the person and work of Christ equally at all times.

Emphases in preaching likewise shift to an extent depending on the subject matter treated. However, we must preach James as a book in light of the entire canon of Scripture. Preachers must remember that they will not preach the Book of James in one sitting. This means that they should keep the biblical goals of preaching set forth elsewhere in Scripture in view while preaching James. Multiple sermons on James should expound each passage with a partial view to the rest of Scripture as it bears on each stage of the argument. Doing so makes Christology more inevitable. We should preach James rather than turning the book into a general Bible study in which we cite numerous other passages. Yet we should preach James as Christian preachers even as we would preach Proverbs in this way.[1]

Psalm 1—a pattern for walking with God

Old Testament preaching presents its own challenges to preachers. In order to preach Christ effectively in Old Testament sermons, preachers must use the tools outlined previously (exegesis, redemptive history, theology, and devotion). I can illustrate these principles by using Psalm 1. Psalm 1 proclaims the blessedness of the man who avoids ungodly counsel and ways because he meditates on God's law day and night (v. 1-2). The result is that he becomes like a stable, well-watered, and fruitful tree (v. 3). He is blessed by contrast to the ungodly, who are like chaff driven by the wind (v. 4-5). In summary, God knows (and loves) the godly person as he walks in the right path, but the ungodly shall perish in their way (v. 6).

An exegetical sermon should follow the structure of the Psalm, enabling the minister to preach the text. Yet exegesis does not lead to Christ here directly, since the text does not include explicit prophecies or promises related to Christ. Redemptive history takes us farther by pointing us to Christ as the ideal righteous man who obeyed the law of God perfectly. Yet the pastor still needs to warn every man and teach every man to present every man perfect in Christ.

Theology demands that Christ is not only the foundation of our justification, but that he is the pattern of our sanctification. The Spirit renews us in God's image in Christ. He uses meditation on God's law, shunning the counsel of the ungodly, and not standing in their paths nor sitting in their seats as means of doing so. Christ is the remedy for our sin where we fail and he is the ground of our perseverance and growth in godliness. He also offers hope to the ungodly.

Read through Christian eyes, this Psalm becomes a pattern for what it means to walk with God, through Christ, by his Spirit.[2] Exegesis should shape the structure of a sermon on Psalm 1. Redemptive history situates the Psalm in its relation to the covenant of grace. Theology becomes a bridge to devotional application in light of the work of the Triune God for us and in us.

Amos: From failure to fulfillment

Preaching the Book of Amos illustrates how to apply the biblical model for preaching Christ to another genre of Old Testament literature. I once attended a conference in which a minister exhorted pastors to preach Christ and a listener later asked him how to preach Christ in a series through Amos. He answered bluntly that most ministers should not preach consecutively through Amos. Surely this answer is wrong, since all Scripture is both profitable and it is able to make us wise for salvation through faith in Christ (2 Timothy 3:15). However, exegesis will not sustain the goals of preaching in relation to preaching Christ through Amos.

As with Psalm 1, the text of Amos should provide the structure for each sermon. Yet Amos 1:1-5:3 denounces the people for sin with no call to repentance until 5:4-15. The threat of the Day of the Lord follows immediately (5:16-27). Chapters 6:1-9:10 resume the prophet's warnings and threats. Only the end of the book (9:11-15) contains a promise of hope through restoring the "tabernacle of David" (cited in Acts 15:16). This is the only clear exegetical handle in the book to lead preachers to preach Christ directly. Retelling the story of redemptive history in every sermon runs the risk of monotony after preaching chapter one. Preaching Christ should never be boring or tedious.

Theology and devotion become the primary tools of preaching Christ throughout Amos. Every denunciation of prophets, priests, and kings should lead us to Christ's fulfillment of these offices by contrast. Every denunciation of sin should drive us to Christ. Christians should grieve over their sins against Christ and the preacher should press unbelievers towards Christ. Amos' call to repentance should drive us to the Spirit of Christ, who enables us to respond appropriately.

Theology and devotion can turn prohibitions into commands and threats into their corresponding promises. If the King of Nineveh inferred God's mercies from his threats (Jonah 3:3-9), then how much more should God's people infer them from Amos? Preaching Christ from Amos will require every skill in a pastor's toolbox to meet the biblical goals of preaching. Yet, according to Paul, they must do so.

Preaching Christ is not always easy, but the first six chapters of this book showed that doing so is part of the biblical definition of preaching. Christian preaching must be distinctively Christian in tone and in content. The goals of preaching in general must set the goals for every particular sermon. Ministers do not need to say all that can be said about Christ in every sermon, but they must have the gospel in view at all times. As Spurgeon wrote, "My brethren, preach Christ, always and evermore. He is the whole gospel."[3] This illustrates preeminently why preaching demands hard work and fervent prayer.

The best thing that you can do for your pastor is to pray that the Spirit would so enflame his heart with Christ's glory that he cannot help but preach Christ in all of his sermons. We should also be patient with our ministers as they wrestle through preaching biblical books that are more challenging than others.

Study Questions

1. What makes the Book of James unusual in the New Testament? How should Christians approach and use this book?
2. Why is preaching Christ harder when preaching the Old Testament?
3. Does preaching Christ from the Old Testament always demand redemptive-historical preaching? Does it mean that we should find Christ directly in every passage of Scripture?
4. How should a Christian relate Christ to Psalm 1? Give an example of another Psalm to which you can apply the same principles.
5. Why should you exercise charity towards your pastor as he preaches through the Old Testament? How can you encourage him as he labors through difficult tasks like this one? How can you pray for him?

12

WHAT SHOULD SERMON APPLICATION LOOK LIKE?

It does not really matter if an archer has good aim if he has no target. He must know what to look for and where to send his arrow if he hopes to hit his mark. His good aim must have an object and he must know how to hit it. Preaching Christ is part of the definition of preaching, but it is not the only task of preachers. Warning every man and teaching every man in order to present every man perfect in Christ (Colossians 1:28) requires wise and specific application.

What should sermon application look like? If I tell my children to do some cleaning in the house, then their version of cleaning and mine may not coincide. If, by contrast, I tell them that I want them to clean their rooms and I show them how to put clothes on hangers, how to make their beds, and how to dust their shelves, then they understand better what I want them to do and how to do it. Sermon application likewise requires specific directions in order to meet its aims.

Application as direction to respond

Application in preaching should direct people to respond in specific ways to the work of the Triune God in redemption. Application must be direct, pointed, specific, searching, and it should address many kinds of hearers.[1]

Application in preaching should be direct. Occasionally, Paul was very direct. He cited "Chloe's household" as the source of his knowledge of the divisions in Corinth (1 Corinthians 1:11). He implored Euodia and Syntyche "to be of the same mind in the Lord" (Philippians 4:2). Such examples are sparing and we should be sparing in following them. We often lack the skill to do so wisely (though I have had to call my children by name twice from the pulpit while mom was out caring for a baby).

Preaching can be more general than this and still be direct. Peter accused his hearers of crucifying Christ and called them to repent (Acts 2:36, 38). He used "you" repeatedly in calling people to repentance (Acts 3:12-26). Paul did the same thing in Acts 13:16-41, 28:17-29 and in virtually all of his recorded sermons. The epistles in the New Testament bear the same character. Sermon application must address people directly in order to qualify as application.

Pointed application

Application in preaching should be pointed, aiming at specific responses. It must aim at the heart.[2] According to the author of Hebrews, people must receive the Word of

God in faith and obedience because it will judge them like a sharp two-edged sword (Hebrews 4:11-13). Paul gave lists of appropriate responses to the gospel in passages like Romans 12, 1 Thessalonians 5:12-19, and others like them. Many people are afraid of such lists because they think that they lead to "legalism." Lists of duties can be abused if we are looking for exhaustive rules for Christian living or if we detach them from their grounding in Christ. Yet Paul assumed that believers needed such lists to make application concrete. Believers need to know what God wants them to do.

Application as specific direction

Application in preaching should include specific directions. Preachers must show people how to respond to pointed application. The New Testament provides many examples of clear directions telling people how to do what God requires them to do. 1 Corinthians 8-10, noted previously, illustrates what this looks like. Paul taught believers the principles that they needed to address the question of eating food offered to idols. However, he also told them how to apply these principles in a variety of circumstances, giving them examples. His teaching on marriage in chapter seven follows the same pattern.

In the Sermon on the Mount, Jesus introduced examples related to some of the Ten Commandments, telling his hearers what they did not mean and showing them how to apply them. "Thou shalt not kill" applies to our hearts, to our speech, and to the need to be reconciled to others (Matthew 5:21-26). His application was not exhaustive, but it was pointed and specific. He added applications to principles.

Applying the commandments to our hearts, speech, and outward behavior applies to all Ten Commandments by implication (see Westminster Larger Catechism 99, which derives rules for interpreting the law from Jesus' example).[3] Without explicit examples of how to apply God's Word believers often desire to obey God without knowing how to do so. When we tell people that they need to meditate on God's law day and night (Psalm 1:1-2) we need to teach them how to do such things.

Preachers should not try to exhaust specific directions in a sermon. Like Christ and Paul, they should provide sufficient examples to give practical shape to biblical teaching, teaching Christians how to think critically about life. Believers need specific directions in preaching.

Searching application

Application in preaching should be searching. This feature of preaching often comes via questions leading to personal reflection. Paul reduced the legalism of the Galatian church to absurdity through a series of questions directing them to reflect on their actions in light of the gospel (Galatians 3:1-9). The author of Hebrews used questions repeatedly to drive his readers to consider the seriousness of apostasy and to flee from it (e.g. Hebrews 2:3, 3:16-19, 9:11-15, 10:26-31, 12:9). Searching questions were his ordinary means of moving his readers to take action.

Searching questions can also lead believers to comfort in Christ, as Paul used them in Romans 8:31-38. As William Perkins noted long ago, sermons require "mental application," teaching us how to meditate as well as what to do.[4] Such questions mark preaching throughout the book of Acts and the epistles of the New Testament. Questions in preaching should drive people to respond to specific applications and directions.

Application made personal

Application in preaching should address all kinds of hearers. Hearers possess different levels of Christian maturity. Some are children in Christ while some are young men and others are fathers (1 John 2:12-14). Some application is relevant to all believers (Ephesians 4:17-5:20). Other application singles out specific groups of hearers, such as husbands and wives (5:22-33), children (6:1-3), fathers (6:4), servants and masters (6:5-9), widows (1 Timothy 5:3-16), wealthy people (6:17-19; James 5:1-6), poor people (James 1:9), women (1 Peter 3:1-6), and others. The Bible addresses officers in their particular responsibilities (1 Peter 5:1-4) and members in relation to their officers (Hebrews 13:7, 17; 1 Thessalonians 5:12-13).

Ministers should also speak directly to converted and to unconverted people as well as to hypocrites and to faithful and doubting Christians. Examples of addressing hearers in different stations of life, levels of maturity, ages, differences of sex, and many other differences appear consistently in the preaching of the Old Testament prophets as well. Almost all of these examples use "you" to people. This makes preaching personal. Addressing specific kinds of hearers in sermons brings direct, pointed, specific, and searching application to bear on everyone hearing the sermon more powerfully.

Sermon application must bear such characteristics because those hearing sermons need to hear Christ directly. Some may object that such application usurps the role of the Holy Spirit, who applies the Word of God to our hearts. While preachers should not embarrass individuals from the pulpit, is this criticism fair? If I tell a child to clean his room but I never teach him what cleaning a room looks like, then will I not frustrate the child and myself rather than help him or her?

The Spirit works through Scripture and through preaching Scripture. The Spirit gives us many biblical examples of very specific application. While not all biblical examples of application are equally direct, pointed, or searching, sermon application should reflect the general pattern of Scripture. This underscores the fact that preaching requires exercising mature spiritual wisdom coupled with prayerful exegetical labor.

The biblical model for sermon application not only teaches us what to expect from preaching. It teaches us many useful lessons about personal evangelism as well.[5] Good sermons that are full of application model for us how to apply Scripture to others. We should learn to bring biblical truths to unbelieving friends and family members directly, pointedly, specifically, and searchingly. We should pray for wisdom in how to apply the gospel to all kinds of people as well. While personal evangelism is not preaching, good preaching can help us grow in personal evangelism. We should take what we learn from Christ through sermons and bring it to others who do not yet know Christ.

∼

Study Questions

1. Why is application a necessary part of preaching? How does application in preaching relate to the Spirit's power at work through preaching?
2. What does it mean for preaching to be direct? How is direct preaching liable to abuse? What should direct preaching look like? Give examples.
3. Why should application in preaching include specific directions? Give examples in which such directions are necessary without raising them to the level of "thus says the Lord."
4. What does it mean for application to be searching? In what specific ways does God search our hearts by using the Scriptures? Give examples.
5. Why is it important for sermons to address

various kinds of hearers? Does this mean that everything in the sermon is for you in particular?
6. How does the character of application in preaching reflect the work of the Triune God through preaching?

HOW SHOULD ALL CHRISTIANS PARTICIPATE IN SERMONS?

When I was in college, I started as a Physics major. I then moved to Chemistry and to Engineering. However, I faced a common obstacle. I could not pass Calculus. While I have many friends who are engineers, my life took a different course. I am interested enough in engineering to glean something when friends tell me about their work projects, but I often don't know how to ask intelligent questions about their projects, let alone to do anything with what I learn.

This book may have a similar feel at some points. It has presented a theology of preaching from Scripture. Because it follows biblical texts, most of its chapters describe what preachers must do rather than what all believers should do. However, preaching is not like engineering. Every Christian needs to understand the theology of preaching in Scripture if for no other reason than that every Christian needs to read, understand, and apply Scripture as they grow in love to God. Christ also designed every Christian to sit under sermons though he will not call all of them to be engineers. In light of these facts, are there ways for all believers to participate in sermons and have a stake in them even when they are not called to be preachers?

This chapter seeks to show that all Christians, and not the preacher only, should participate actively in the preparation, delivery, and reception of sermons. While this may sound ambiguous and surprising initially, drawing broadly from biblical principles shows how and why we all have a role to play in preaching, whether or not we are preachers.

Sermon preparation as an act of the church

All Christians should be involved in sermon preparation. Preachers are Christ's gift to the church for her protection, edification, growth, and unity in the Lord (Ephesians 4:11-16). We must recognize that the sermon is an act of the congregation as well as of the pastor.[1] Lloyd-Jones went so far as to say "that the primary task of the Church and of the Christian minister is the preaching of the Word of God."[2] As we have seen, God gifts preachers for their task through Christ by the Spirit. The church recognizes gifted men by electing them to office and presbyteries (elders) and commissions them for their work.

Church members do not simply elect preachers to do their work, leaving the church with nothing else to do. The primary means of assisting pastors in sermon preparation is prayer (Romans 15:30-32; 2 Thessalonians 3:1). We should cultivate private and family habits of praying for preaching, but we should prioritize corporate prayer as well (John 14:12-14; Acts 4:32-31). The sad reality that prayer meetings are ordinarily the worst attended meeting of the church reflects the fact that the church has often lost her sense of responsibility in relation to sermons.

We should pray for preachers in light of the biblical definitions and goals of preaching. We should pray privately and corporately that the Spirit would accompany our pastors in their studies in order to achieve the aims of preaching.[3] Do we pray that the Spirit would increase love for Christ in our ministers so that they would preach him devotionally? Do we pray that the Lord would grant them the skills needed to fulfill the duties of their office? Do we pray that Christ would give them the ability to apply their sermons wisely, warning every man and teaching every man in order to present every man perfect in Christ (Colossians 1:28)? The role of church members in sermon preparation through prayer is equally vital (if not more so) as the pastor's prayers throughout his studies. Through private and corporate prayer, we participate in the preparation of sermons.

Hearing the sermon

All Christians should be engaged in the delivery of sermons. We should prepare ourselves to receive the preaching of the Word. Since the Spirit uses the reading, but especially the preaching of the Word, as an effectual means of our salvation, "we must attend thereunto with diligence, preparation and prayer; receive it with faith and love, lay it up in our hearts, and practice it in our lives" (WSC 90).

We must take diligent heed to what we hear (Luke 8:18), searching the Scriptures to see whether these things are so (Acts 17:11). We must prepare to hear the Word with prayer, expecting to hear Christ in the sermon (Romans 10:14). We must receive the Word from Christ with faith and love (1 Thessalonians 2:13), holding fast to what is good (1 Thessalonians 5:21). We must lay up the Scriptures in our hearts and practice their teachings in our lives, being doers of the Word and not hearers only (James 1:22). We should also pray for the pastor while he preaches, just as the people prayed for Zacharias while he served in the temple (Luke 1:10).

Beyond the preaching

All Christians should promote the reception of sermons. Our work does not stop in expecting to hear Christ through preaching. Our duties as listeners extend to ourselves and to others beyond the time of preaching itself. We should strive to increase the profit of the sermon by referring to it in conversation and in family worship. We should be ready to highlight what is good in the sermon and to overlook any faults in the preacher. The best way to kill the profit of sermons is to build prejudices against ministers. We should prevent such prejudices in ourselves and others by holding fast to what is good and rejecting what is not (1 Thessalonians 5:21-22).

Evangelism through preaching

We should prayerfully invite others to come and hear Christ through sermons just as his early disciples invited others to "come and see" Christ for themselves (John 1:39-41). Christ proclaims the good news of God's righteousness in the assembly of the saints (Psalm 40:9-10). Part of our evangelism consists in calling others to magnify the Lord with us (Psalm 34:3) so that under the preaching of the Word the thoughts of their hearts would be revealed and they might know that God is truly among us (1 Corinthians 14:25).

Attending preaching

We should sit regularly under the preaching of the Word in both services on the Lord's Day, if our churches have two services. Attendance at evening worship is often poor, second only to prayer meetings. These things are connected. Instead of asking where the Bible requires us to come to evening worship, should we not come to both services, in part, because of the high importance the Bible attaches to preaching? Those who pray privately and corporately for pastors, who engage in spiritual labor to profit from sermons, and who want to help others do so are more likely to look for opportunities to hear sermons. For some, the question is whether they can attend evening worship, but for many the question is whether they desire to be there. We should use every means at our disposal to ensure that we receive sermons profitably and help others do so.

Effective preaching depends as much on the labors of the congregation as it does on the labors of preachers. The purposes of preaching should set the tone for our prayers for the preached Word, especially in our prayer meetings. Our aim in listening to sermons should be for our own salvation and for that of others (1 Thessalonians 5:15). We should not be passive observers with regard to sermon preparation, delivery, and reception. We have an active and vital part to play in preaching, even if we never deliver a sermon or stand behind a pulpit.

∾

Study Questions

1. Why should all Christians study preaching, whether or not they are called to preach? How can studying preaching help you understand parts of the Bible itself better?
2. How can we involve our families in sermon preparation? What would this look like in our daily or weekly practices?
3. How should we prepare ourselves to hear and receive the preaching of the Word? How can we help others do the same things?
4. Why is prayer so important in relation to the preaching and hearing of the Word? What are

some ways that we can develop good habits of praying for the preaching and hearing of the Word?
5. How can the Lord's Day help us benefit from the preached Word? What are some reasons that we should attend evening and morning worship on the Lord's Day?
6. In what ways does effective preaching depend on the congregation as much as on the minister? How can we encourage such thinking in our local churches?

14

WHAT IF I SIT UNDER PREACHING THAT DOES NOT MATCH THE BIBLICAL MODEL?

We live in an imperfect world. Those who love their jobs will still be weary in them at times. Those who have obedient children with sweet dispositions will still be frustrated by them at times. We can love exercise and get injured while doing it. The best marriages bring added cares and worries both to wives and to husbands. Every human activity and relationship in this world is affected by sin and admits improvement.

Preaching is no exception. Preachers are weak and imperfectly sanctified men.[1] They hold the treasure of gospel ministry in earthen vessels (2 Corinthians 4:7). There is not a just man on earth who does good and does not sin (Ecclesiastes 7:20). Not many should be teachers because we all fail in many things (James 3:1).

In light of such facts, Jeremiah and Amos both doubted their abilities to fulfill their prophetic offices (Jeremiah 1:6; Amos 7:14-15) and Paul asked who could be sufficient for these things (2 Corinthians 2:16). Yet the

Lord rebuked Jeremiah (Jeremiah 1:7), Amos spoke God's words (Amos 7:16), and God made Paul sufficient for his task (2 Corinthians 3:5). No preacher will fulfill all the ends of preaching perfectly any more than any Christian can obey God perfectly in this life. All believers, including preachers, must press onward toward the upward call of God in Christ (Philippians 3:14).

In light of the previous thirteen chapters, what should you do if the preaching you sit under every Lord's Day falls short of the biblical definition and model of preaching? This section provides encouragements to exercise discernment, charity, and patience in dealing with the faults of preachers.

Exercise discernment

We must exercise discernment in dealing with faults in preaching. If the preacher's flaws are fatal, such as denying or neglecting cardinal doctrines of the faith, then it is time to look for a new church. I know people who sat for years under ministers without knowing that their ministers denied Christ's deity because he never spoke to the issue from the pulpit. These preachers sinned by commission by denying Christ doctrinally. However, they sinned in preaching their sermons by omission. Many of their hearers were immature believers who did not know the difference until they heard better sermons elsewhere.

Other flaws in preaching are unintentional. Sometimes after preaching, I have told my wife that it was as though I was standing in the pulpit watching a train wreck happen before my eyes. Preachers can have all the right aims in preaching, working hard on their sermons, and everything seems to fall apart regardless of these facts. This leads to the next point concerning charity.

Hear with charity

We must receive the preached Word charitably. Preachers need encouragement as much as all believers do. Someone once told me that they loved their pastor and profited from his sermons greatly, but that they would never tell him so because they did not want him to become prideful. I responded that they do not want him to despair and quit either.

We all need to know that the Lord is using us for his glory. Jeremiah and Ezekiel despaired when no one seemed to receive their messages (Jeremiah 4:10; 12:1-4; 20:7-10; Ezekiel 9:8; 20:49). Elijah wanted to quit because he thought that he alone remained faithful to the Lord (1 Kings 18:22; 19:10). Paul regarded faithful hearers as his crown and joy in the Lord (Philippians 4:1; 1 Thessalonians 2:19). Preachers want to know that Christ is being formed in us (Galatians 4:19) and we should tell our ministers when Christ is using them in our lives. Love also covers a multitude of sins (Proverbs 10:12; 1 Peter 4:8).

Bearing one another's burdens includes helping preachers bear theirs (Galatians 6:2). We can do so by adopting a charitable attitude toward our preachers and looking for what is good in their sermons.

Hear with patience

We must be patient with our preachers as we sit under their ministries. For that matter, we must be patient with everyone (1 Thessalonians 5:14). Ministers will grow in their gifts for preaching as they use them and we must give them room to grow.

We should pray through the nature and goals of preaching, outlined in this book, to the end that the Lord would shape the thoughts, affections, and practices of our pastors in light of them. Some preachers do not believe that they need to preach Christ or apply him directly to their audiences. We should pray that the Lord would convince and convict them. Others need more years to develop their skill in preaching. We need to be patient, looking to the Lord to develop them as preachers. Leaving a church due to faulty preaching should be our last resort rather than our first one. As Pierre Marcel wrote,

> If a believer, feeling authorized by what has just been said, is inclined to conclude that his pastor does not preach, let him know that he, a believer, and the Church with him bear more responsibility for it than the pastor himself. We have not spoken of the Spirit whom the preacher alone is to receive, but the Spirit of the Church, whom the Church, i.e. each believer, entreats and from whom he simply receives his share. The lot of a people of God is to hear the preaching of

the word, which people he wishes to bless by hearing and answering their prayers.[2]

Praying always

We should first pray for the preacher, then talk to him about his preaching if necessary, and then talk to the elders of the church. We should leave a church only when the situation appears to be beyond remedy. In many cases we may have nowhere else to go and we must remain gracious, patient, and prayerful.

We must cultivate a positive attitude towards preaching and preachers, since there is always something praiseworthy in the work of a preacher who truly loves Christ. We must beware of complaining and grumbling about the faults in our ministers. Satan will use such things to create an attitude of bitterness in us. This often results in becoming predisposed to criticize sermons sharply no matter who is preaching.

Using discernment, developing a charitable attitude, and exercising patience under preaching are vital in dealing with the faults of preachers. Such things are important aspects of our sanctification as well. How we respond to sermons affects how we live as Christians in other areas of life. At the same time, recognizing that even the best men in the pulpit are men at best should increase our fervency in prayer for preachers as they preach. In many cases, the church's view of preaching requires a theological overhaul in light of the texts treated in this book.

As we pray for the spread of the gospel through the church, we must pray for more biblical preaching. The preaching of the Word extends Christ's ministry to the church and to the world. We need to know what preaching is, how it should be done, and what its goals are in order to know what to expect from sermons and how to pray for the spread of Christ's kingdom.

The good news is that, as Christians, we are getting better and our preachers are getting better. We are not only affected by remaining sin in everything we do. We are shining more brightly until the perfect day (Proverbs 4:18). We are being transformed from glory to glory by beholding the glory of God in the face of Jesus Christ (2 Corinthians 3:18). We should have a positive attitude and expectation for our own growth in Christ and we should have the same attitude towards those who preach the gospel to us. Will this not affect how we communicate with preachers and elders about the preaching of the Word?

Study Questions

1. How should we exercise discernment under the preached Word? Why is it important to be well-informed biblically about what true preaching is?
2. How can we exercise charity towards preachers

as we hear sermons? Why is it important to encourage preachers in what they are doing right? Give some examples of how you can encourage your preacher in his preaching.
3. Why is it a temptation for preachers to quit? How should this affect our dealings with them about faults in their preaching?
4. How can we avoid developing a bitter spirit under preaching? How can we cultivate a positive attitude towards preachers?
5. How should a positive view of sanctification affect our expectations in the Christian life for ourselves and for our preachers?

15

CONCLUSION

Profiting from sermons requires more than good listening skills. We must understand what preaching is, how it should be done, and why it is necessary in order to know what to expect from God through it. Many ministers preach, and many more believers hear, without developing a theology of preaching from Scripture. Yet as preaching stands at the heart of the life of the church, it is important for all believers to know what it is and what it should look like.

This book seeks to exemplify some of the principles of sermon application in written form. It does not give practical examples of every possible scenario on preaching (any more than Christ did in the Sermon on the Mount). It has set forth principles from Scripture, adding practical examples to help clarify them and to allow room for applying them in similar cases.

In light of biblical texts examined in this book, many debates over the method of preaching appear to be off base. They often begin with arguments based on accepted methods borrowed from modern exegesis and biblical theology instead of with biblical definitions. Both areas of study provide useful tools for preachers, but it is easy to follow such methods (or a combination of them) without defining what preaching is from Scripture first. Should not the biblical definition of preaching, with its Scriptural goals, determine the tools that preachers should use in preaching as well as how they should use them?

In light of its biblical definition, we should understand that preaching is hard work that requires fervent prayer. It is not particularly difficult to read a pile of Bible commentaries and to summarize for others what we read. Yet preaching requires great spiritual wisdom to explain and to apply biblical passages, aiming to preach Christ's person and work, seeking to apply him to every hearer, and using a variety of tools to do so. Preachers need spiritual gifts, acute skill, and continual exercise to preach in this way. Clear thinking is required to retain Christ's incarnation as the theological bridge between the Triune God and all other things as they relate to God. This is preaching Christ, in demonstration of the Spirit and of power, to the Father's glory.

The practical and experiential dimensions of preaching require more than theological and intellectual coherence. Preachers must know and love Christ themselves if they would help others know and love him. Their preaching must flow from their own daily communion with Christ if they hope in their sermons to plead with people on Christ's behalf to be reconciled to God.

Above all, preaching is not a spectator sport. The greatest gift that all Christians can give to their ministers is to pray that the Spirit would fulfill the ends of preaching through their sermons. Marcel wrote,

> If every pastor knew and felt that the congregation was praying and that each member had prayed, that the congregation was supporting him, interceding for him, that each member had benevolent feelings for the man whom God had given to instruct in salvation, that each one loved him in God, what preacher would not feel himself a new man? And whose preaching would not be transformed?[1]

Preaching is not for the faint of heart. Just as not everyone has the skill to be an engineer, so not everyone has the skill to preach the Word. There is no shame in recognizing that Christians have different gifts and callings. We need more gifted men in the pulpit and we need more devoted church members praying for them. Yet gifts are not static realities admitting no growth. Fervent prayer can make mediocre preachers great and great preachers better. We can make good preachers better through our labors. Moreover, knowing what preaching is helps us profit more from sermons. This theology of preaching should shape how we listen as we learn to love Christ better through listening to sermons.

Study Questions

1. Why are many current debates over method in preaching off base? Give some examples. What is often missing in such debates?
2. Why is preaching such hard work? How are preaching and Christian devotion interrelated? What can these things teach us about Christian living in general?
3. Why did Marcel argue that hearers are, in some sense, more responsible for the preaching than the preacher? Is this true? How should we respond to this idea?
4. Why is preaching not for the faint of heart? How should this affect how the church evaluates a candidate's gifting and call for ministry?

16

APPENDIX: FOLLOWING SERMON STRUCTURE

When our children first started taking notes on sermons, they wrote down as many bits of information as fast as they could. While the phrases they wrote down came from the sermon, an outside observer would see the notes as a random collection of statements. This practice can prove true for adults as well. It is possible to listen to sermons in a disjointed way in which we look for points that strike us instead of following an extended train of thought. Individual ideas in a sermon should fit into a unified whole. Learning how to follow the structure and arguments of a sermon can help us think through passages of Scripture better as well as retain what we hear more effectively. There are several things that we should look for in sermons in order to achieve these goals.[1]

First, identify the main point of the sermon. The point of a sermon should consist of more than jumping into the next passage in a sequence of others. A thesis statement, or main proposition, should guide sermons.

This statement distills the heart of the text preached into a single sentence. For example, Paul's proposition guiding the book of Romans is that he is not ashamed of the gospel because it is the power of God for salvation (Romans 1:17). The rest of the book explains why this was the case and how readers should respond to the gospel message.

Genesis 3:15 serves virtually as a thesis statement for the entire Bible, in which Christ's victory over sin and Satan for his people would set the tone for the rest of redemptive history. Smaller sections within almost all biblical books, Proverbs and a few others excepted, form arguments or narratives that are part of a larger whole. Each of them has their own main point that contributes to the movement of the book.

As preachers identify the main point of the section of Scripture on which they are preaching, usually in their introductions, our ears should be open to listen for the main point. This helps us understand individual sections of Scripture better and enables us to identify the unifying theme that ties all subsequent ideas in the sermon together.

Second, look for the purpose of the sermon. Why did Paul want to preach the gospel to those in Rome (Romans 1:15)? Positively, because in it the righteousness of God is revealed from faith to faith for the salvation of those who believe (1:17). Negatively, because the wrath of God is revealed from heaven against all ungodliness and unrighteousness of men (1:18).

Paul's purpose was to explain the gospel for the salvation of all people. We can often locate the purpose of a sermon by asking the question, "Why is the teaching of this text important?" The purpose of the sermon should closely mirror the main point of the text. It moves us from summarizing what we should expect to learn to why we should care about learning it. Like the main proposition, the purpose of a sermon should appear in its introduction. Looking for the purpose of the sermon creates an expectation in us to know what we should learn from this particular passage.

Third, discern the flow of thought in a sermon. Ask yourself why the main points of the sermon prove its main proposition and fulfill its purpose. If biblical texts form arguments or press narratives forward, then the points of the sermon should ordinarily build these arguments and pull us through the meaning of biblical narratives.

The Bible is not a random collection of memorable verses. Scripture reasons with us and leads us to conclusions; sermons should do this too. Ask how each point of the sermon promotes the main point of the sermon. If the preacher expounds his text well, then this will help you think through the reasoning present in the text more easily.

If the sermon is not as clear on this point as it should be, then you can still apply this counsel to think through the progression of thought in the text preached on your own. At the very least, the Lord is using the sermon to direct your attention to that text today and, whether structured well or poorly, he is using the sermon to help you meditate on the text.

Fourth, take note of the doctrines and applications in the sermon. Every sermon should teach us something about God, about ourselves, and about everything else in relation to both. We should ask ourselves how this sermon directs us to contemplate such things. Every sermon should teach us to believe or do something as well. Beware of only thinking about others who you know "need to hear this."

As Jonathan Edwards reminded himself weekly, you should hear all sermons for yourself, even if you do not think that there is anything "in it for you." God's Word always has something to say to us by way of doctrine and application. We should expect sermons to teach us how to marvel at God's beauties and serve him more cheerfully.

Fifth, use the conclusion of the sermon to solidify the main point and primary application of the text. While pastors should address many kinds of hearers in many different conditions of life, we should not lose sight of applications that we all hold in common. Though the sermon should address us as individuals, it should tie us together as well. It is useful to ask ourselves what "main takeaway" the pastor wants all of us to grasp in his message, or more importantly, what takeaway God wants us to grasp from his Word. Hopefully these two things will coincide. Doing such things drives us back to the main proposition and purpose of the sermon now that we have seen how the preacher led us there through the text.

Learning how to identify and follow sermon structure

makes the entire sermon and the text on which it is based more memorable. Yet what if the structure of the sermon is not clear? Clarity in structure is certainly something that pastors need to develop and that some are better naturally at doing than others. If this is a difficulty that you face in your congregation, then maybe this appendix can be a starting point for fruitful conversation with the pastor. Yet remember to be positive, thankful, and kind in doing so. Whether the preacher makes the structure of a text clear to us or not, we can still profit from his sermons more effectively if we apply the advice given here. The Lord may bless these means to help us clarify what is unclear. In any case, doing so will help us think through the text preached better and learn from it more fully.

∽

Study Questions

1. How can we identify the main point of a sermon? How is the main point related to the purpose of a sermon?
2. How should the flow of thought in a sermon relate to the flow of thought in the text? How can you use the flow of thought in the sermon to help you identify the flow of thought in the text, even when the sermon does not do this adequately?
3. How can we expand the application of the

Appendix: Following Sermon Structure

sermon beyond what the pastor gives to us? Do we have any responsibility in this area that goes beyond the responsibility of the preacher in his preaching?

4. How can the conclusion of the sermon help us tie together all of the parts of the sermon? How does this help us remember what we have heard and learned?

5. What responsibility does this material on sermon structure place on ministers? What does it place on congregations? How can we show gratitude for what is right in the sermon even when sermon structure and aims may be somewhat unclear?

SELECT BIBLIOGRAPHY

Augustine. *Expositions on the Book of Psalms*. Edited by Philip Schaff. Vol. 8. Nicene and Post-Nicene Fathers: First Series. Peabody, MA: Hendrickson Publishers, 2004.
Azurdia, Arturo G. *Spirit Empowered Preaching: Involving the Holy Spirit in Your Ministry*. Fearn, Ross-shire, Great Britain: Mentor, 1998.
Bates, William. *The Works of William Bates*. 4 vols. Harrisonburg, VA: Sprinkle Publications, 1990.
Calvin, John. *Institutes of the Christian Religion*. Edited by John T. McNeill. Translated by Ford Lewis Battles. Vol. XX–XXI. 2 vols. Library of Christian Classics. Philadelphia: Westminster Press, 1960.
Capill, Murray. *The Heart Is the Target: Preaching Practical Application from Every Text*. Phillipsburg, N.J.: P & R Publishing, 2015.
Carrick, John. *The Imperative of Preaching: A Theology of Sacred Rhetoric*. Carlisle: Banner of Truth, 2002.
Chrysostom, John. *Homilies on the Acts of the Apostles and*

the Epistle to the Romans. Vol. 11. Nicene and Post-Nicene Fathers: First Series. Peabody, MA: Hendrickson Publishers, 2004.

———. *Homilies on the Epistles of Paul to the Corinthians*. Edited by Philip Schaff. Vol. 12. Nicene and Post-Nicene Fathers: First Series. Peabody. MA: Hendrickson Publishers, 2004.

Crowe, Brandon D., and Carl R. Trueman, eds. *The Essential Trinity: New Testament Foundations and Practical Relevance*. Phillipsburg, NJ, 2017.

Dabney, Robert Lewis *Evangelical Eloquence: A Course of Lectures on Preaching*. Edinburgh: Banner of Truth, 1999.

Davis, Dale Ralph. *The Word Became Fresh: How to Preach from Old Testament Narrative Texts*. Fearn, Ross-shire, Scotland: Mentor, 2006.

Ferguson, Sinclair B. *Some Pastors and Teachers: Reflecting a Biblical Vision of What Every Minister Is Called to Be*. Banner of Truth, 2017.

James, John Angell. *An Earnest Ministry*. Edinburgh: Banner of Truth, 1993.

Knox, David Broughton. *Sent by Jesus: Some Aspects of Christian Ministry Today*. Edinburgh: Banner of Truth, 1992.

Lloyd-Jones, David Martyn. *Preaching and Preachers*. Grand Rapids, MI: Zondervan, 1972.

Manton, Thomas. *The Complete Works*. London: Nisbet, 1870.

Marcel, Pierre-Charles. *The Relevance of Preaching*. Translated by Rob Roy McGregor. Grand Rapids, MI: Baker, 1977.

Martin, Albert N. *Preaching in the Holy Spirit*. Grand Rapids, Mich.: Reformation Heritage Books, 2011.

Mastricht, Peter van. *The Best Method of Preaching: The Use of Theoretical-Practical Theology*. Translated by Todd Rester. Grand Rapids, MI: Reformation Heritage Books, 2013.

McGraw, Ryan M. *How Do Preaching and Corporate Prayer Work Together?* Cultivating Biblical Godliness. Grand Rapids, MI: Reformation Heritage Books, 2014.

———. *The Day of Worship: Reassessing the Christian Life in Light of the Sabbath*. Grand Rapids, MI: Reformation Heritage Books, 2011.

McIlvaine, Charles P. *Preaching Christ: The Heart of Gospel Ministry*. Edinburgh: Banner of Truth Trust, 2003.

Murray, David P. *How Sermons Work*. Darlington, England: EP Books, 2011.

Olyott, Stuart, ed. *Ministering Like the Master: Three Messages for Today's Preachers*. Edinburgh: Banner of Truth, 2003.

Perkins, William. *A Warning Against the Idolatrie of the Last Times and an Instruction Touching Religious, or Diuine Worship*. Cambridge, 1601.

———. *The Art of Prophesying*. Edinburgh: Banner of Truth, 1996.

Sanders, Fred. *The Triune God*. New Studies in Dogmatics. Grand Rapids, MI: Zondervan, 2016.

Spurgeon, Charles H. *Lectures to My Students*. Pasadena, TX: Pilgrim Publications, 1990.

Turretin, Francis *Institutes of Elenctic Theology*. Edited by

James T. Dennison. Translated by George Musgrave Giger. 3 vols. Phillipsburg, N.J.: P&R Publishing, 1992.

Webster, John. "The Place of Christology in Systematic Theology." In *The Oxford Handbook of Christology*, edited by Francesca Aran Murphy, 628–48. New York: Oxford University Press, 2015.

NOTES

Introduction

1. David Martyn Lloyd-Jones, *Preaching and Preachers* (Grand Rapids, MI: Zondervan, 1972), 11.
2. Stuart Olyott, ed., *Ministering Like the Master: Three Messages for Today's Preachers* (Edinburgh: Banner of Truth, 2003).

1. What is Preaching?

1. As Marcel wrote in relation to the peculiar vocabulary of Scripture, "Clearly, it is not a problem of vocabulary but of truth. *Evil* is not sin; *liberation from evil* is not redemption; *eternal life* is not resurrection; a *change in morals* is not regeneration; a *progress in morals* is not sanctification, etc. Wherever words are changed, ideas are altered, and instead of truth falsehood is taught." Pierre-Charles Marcel, *The Relevance of Preaching*, trans. Rob Roy McGregor (Grand Rapids, MI: Baker, 1977), 83.
2. "Every Christian should be able to give an account of why he is a Christian; but that does not mean that every Christian is meant to preach." Lloyd-Jones, *Preaching and Preachers*, 102.
3. John Chrysostom, *Homilies on the Epistles of Paul to the Corinthians*, ed. Philip Schaff, vol. 12, Nicene and Post-Nicene Fathers: First Series (Peabody, MA: Hendrickson Publishers, 2004), 336.

2. Why is Preaching Necessary?

1. Lloyd-Jones, *Preaching and Preachers*, 119.
2. David Broughton Knox, *Sent by Jesus: Some Aspects of Christian Ministry Today* (Edinburgh: Banner of Truth, 1992), 15.
3. John Chrysostom, *Homilies on the Acts of the Apostles and the Epistle to*

the Romans, vol. 11, Nicene and Post-Nicene Fathers: First Series (Peabody, MA: Hendrickson Publishers, 2004), 478.

3. How Should Preaching be Done?

1. See the chapter bearing this title in Olyott, *Ministering like the Master*, 1–33.
2. Charles H. Spurgeon, *Lectures to My Students* (Pasadena, TX: Pilgrim Publications, 1990), 83.
3. John Carrick, *The Imperative of Preaching: A Theology of Sacred Rhetoric* (Carlisle: Banner of Truth, 2002), 130.
4. William Perkins, *The Art of Prophesying* (Edinburgh: Banner of Truth, 1996), 79.
5. The best exegetical treatment of that I have read on this subject is Arturo G. Azurdia, *Spirit Empowered Preaching: Involving the Holy Spirit in Your Ministry* (Fearn, Ross-shire, Great Britain: Mentor, 1998).
6. Dabney makes this point clearly and helpfully. See Robert Lewis Dabney, *Evangelical Eloquence: A Course of Lectures on Preaching* (Edinburgh: Banner of Truth, 1999), 114–16.
7. Albert N Martin, *Preaching in the Holy Spirit* (Grand Rapids, Mich.: Reformation Heritage Books, 2011), 7.

4. What are the Proper Aims of Preaching?

1. William Perkins, *A Warning Against the Idolatrie of the Last Times and an Instruction Touching Religious, or Diuine Worship.* (Cambridge, 1601), 152.
2. "Although God is able to complete the number of the elect in an instant, we contend that he has chosen for that purpose the ministry of the word and entrusted to it that task. The business of the Church is to obey the command which has been given to her and to have confidence in the promise received. The question, 'What is God able to do?' is absolutely not to be confused with the question 'What is commanded of us in the promise made to the Church?'" Marcel, *The Relevance of Preaching*, 44.
3. John Webster, "The Place of Christology in Systematic Theology,"

in *The Oxford Handbook of Christology*, ed. Francesca Aran Murphy (New York: Oxford University Press, 2015), 615–16.
4. John Angell James, *An Earnest Ministry* (Edinburgh: Banner of Truth, 1993).

5. What are the Spirit's Aims in Preaching?

1. Francis Turretin wrote a theological text that bears this title because it teaches truth by refuting false doctrine. Francis Turretin, *Institutes of Elenctic Theology*, ed. James T Dennison, trans. George Musgrave Giger, 3 vols. (Phillipsburg, N.J.: P&R Publishing, 1992).
2. I am indebted to Marco Ribeiro for the content of this concluding paragraph.

6. How Does Preaching Relate to the Missions of the Persons of the Trinity?

1. Michael Reeves observes, "Surprisingly little has been written on the Trinity and preaching, and standard textbooks on preaching tend not to give much –if any – time to explaining how the Trinity should inform the preacher's task." Brandon D. Crowe and Carl R. Trueman, eds., *The Essential Trinity: New Testament Foundations and Practical Relevance* (Phillipsburg, NJ, 2017), 289.
2. For a treatment of trinitarian theology built on the processions and missions of the divine persons, see Fred Sanders, *The Triune God*, New Studies in Dogmatics (Grand Rapids, MI: Zondervan, 2016).
3. Crowe and Trueman, *The Essential Trinity*, 291.

7. What are the Proper Methods for Preaching Christ? (1)

1. For an excellent (and entertaining) model of preaching OT narratives, see Dale Ralph Davis, *The Word Became Fresh: How to Preach*

from Old Testament Narrative Texts (Fearn, Ross-shire, Scotland: Mentor, 2006).
2. I am indebted, in part, to Marco Ribeiro for the content of this concluding paragraph.

8. What are the Proper Methods for Preaching Christ? (2)

1. William Bates, *The Works of William Bates*, 4 vols. (Harrisonburg, VA: Sprinkle Publications, 1990).
2. Charles P. McIlvaine, *Preaching Christ: The Heart of Gospel Ministry* (Edinburgh: Banner of Truth Trust, 2003), 39.
3. I adopted this paragraph from Ben Castle's proposed draft of it with some modifications of my own.

9. What Are the Proper Methods for Preaching Christ? (3)

1. Sinclair B. Ferguson, *Some Pastors and Teachers: Reflecting a Biblical Vision of What Every Minister Is Called to Be* (Banner of Truth, 2017), 670.
2. John Calvin, *Institutes of the Christian Religion*, ed. John T. McNeill, trans. Ford Lewis Battles, vol. XX–XXI, Library of Christian Classics (Philadelphia: Westminster Press, 1960), 544. Book 3, chapter 2, section 1.
3. Ferguson, *Some Pastors and Teachers*, 671.

11. Is Preaching Christ Always Inherent to Preaching?

1. For examples of preaching Christ throughout James, see Thomas Manton, *A Practical Exposition of James*, in, *The Complete Works* (London: Nisbet, 1870), vol. 4.
2. Though his methods were a bit allegorical, Augustine provides useful examples of how to preach this Psalm in light of the Trinity.

Augustine, *Expositions on the Book of Psalms*, ed. Philip Schaff, vol. 8, Nicene and Post-Nicene Fathers: First Series (Peabody, MA: Hendrickson Publishers, 2004), 1.
3. Spurgeon, *Lectures to My Students*, 82.

12. What Should Sermon Application Look Like?

1. My favorite treatment of these categories of application using biblical examples remains Carrick, *The Imperative of Preaching*.
2. Murray Capill, *The Heart Is the Target: Preaching Practical Application from Every Text* (Phillipsburg, N.J.: P & R Publishing, 2015).
3. For an example of applying these principles to the fourth commandment, see Ryan M. McGraw, *The Day of Worship: Reassessing the Christian Life in Light of the Sabbath* (Grand Rapids, MI: Reformation Heritage Books, 2011).
4. Perkins, *The Art of Prophesying*, 64.
5. I an grateful to Marco Ribeiro for this point.

13. How Should All Christians Participate in Sermons?

1. For an expansion of this point, see Marcel, *The Relevance of Preaching*, 101–2.
2. Lloyd-Jones, *Preaching and Preachers*, 19.
3. Ryan M. McGraw, *How Do Preaching and Corporate Prayer Work Together?*, Cultivating Biblical Godliness (Grand Rapids, MI: Reformation Heritage Books, 2014).

14. What if I Sit Under Preaching that Does not Match the Biblical Model?

1. Calvin, *Institutes of the Christian Religion*, XX–XXI:1054. Book 4, chapter 3, section 1.
2. Marcel, *The Relevance of Preaching*, 101–2.

15. Conclusion

1. Marcel, 102.

16. Appendix: Following Sermon Structure

1. For a recent and an older example of how to think through the structure of a sermon, see David P. Murray, *How Sermons Work* (Darlington, England: EP Books, 2011); Peter van Mastricht, *The Best Method of Preaching: The Use of Theoretical-Practical Theology*, trans. Todd Rester (Grand Rapids: Reformation Heritage Books, 2013). While I do not believe that we should follow Mastricht's sermon structure exactly today, he still gives us helpful examples of various parts of sermons and what to look for in them.